How to Discover
Your Personal Mission

John Monbourquette

How to Discover
Your Personal Mission

DARTON·LONGMAN+TODD

First published in Great Britain in 2003 by
Darton, Longman and Todd Ltd
1 Spencer Court
140–142 Wandsworth High Street
London SW18 4JJ

First published in French in 1997 by Novalis. English edition first published in 2001 by Novalis, Saint Paul University, Ottawa, Canada and Twenty-Third Publications.

ISBN 0–232–52452–1

A catalogue record for this book is available from the British Library.

Cover design: Blair Turner
Cover photograph: Sarah Platt
Layout: Blaine Hermann

Printed and bound in Great Britain by
The Cromwell Press, Trowbridge, Wiltshire

Happy are those
whose strength you are:
their hearts are set
upon the pilgrimage!

Psalm 84

Acknowledgments

For the original French version of this book, I am grateful to Father Jacques Croteau, my friend and colleague, who so kindly collaborated with me on my writing project. He generously agreed not only to review the text for style and clarity, but also to give a judicious critique of the ideas. Pauline Vertefeuille graciously offered to reread the text with her practised journalist's eye, emphasizing key ideas. Once again, I had the pleasure of seeing the French text edited by Josée Latulippe. I knew it was in good hands, for she handled it with the same care as she would her own work.

For this English edition, I would like to thank Ferdinanda Van Gennip for her thoughtful translation, and Bernadette Gasslein for her careful editing of the text.

About the author

John Monbourquette is a psychotherapist, best-selling author and Roman Catholic priest. While he has both taught high school and worked as a parish priest, his principal interest has been in the relationship between spirituality and psychology. His graduate studies in theology and psychology and his doctoral studies in psychology at the International College of Los Angeles have enabled him to pursue these interests both in the academic world, where he was for many years a professor in the Pastoral Institute of Saint Paul University, Ottawa, and in his own private practice as a pastoral psychologist. His special areas of interest include forgiveness, self-esteem, male violence, the dynamics of grief, and accompanying the dying.

He has given hundreds of conferences on these topics in Canada and Europe to both professional and lay audiences. He is the author (under his French name, Jean Monbourquette) of eight books in French; these books have been translated into nine languages. In addition to *How to Discover Your Personal Mission,* four of these *(How to Love Again: Moving from Grief to Growth,* which has sold over 165,000 copies in six languages around the world; *How to Befriend Your Shadow: Welcoming Your Unloved Side; How to Forgive: A Step-by-Step Guide;* and *Growing Through Loss: A Handbook for Grief Support Groups)* are available in English. Monbourquette is co-author of three other books and has written many articles for professional journals.

TABLE OF CONTENTS

A hospital psychologist once confided to me that the greater part of her time was spent not in listening to patients but in attending to the emotional stress of her colleagues. Most of them questioned the meaning of their existence: "What's the point of living? Does my work really help anyone or change anything? Is there anything more to life than eat-work-sleep?" For many of us, a great existential void has replaced the meanings of life offered by traditional religions and humanist philosophies. I therefore felt it was important to present to readers my reflections on the search for meaning in life, specifically by providing the tools that will enable you to discover your personal mission. Discovering your personal mission truly helps to give meaning to your daily actions and experiences. Knowing the "why" of your existence offers you three important elements of personal fulfillment: your life has meaning, you experience inner unity, and your activity is focused.

WHO SHOULD READ THIS BOOK?

The main purpose of this book is to accompany people who are struggling with life's transitions, whether these have been chosen or not. Sooner or later, we all go through transitions. Many of us live through them without having been sufficiently prepared or initiated: adolescents are catapulted into young adulthood, adults are confronted by mid-life, parents suddenly face the "empty nest," workers begin retirement, elderly people see the end of their lives approaching. These turning points that announce a major life change make all of us ask ourselves some important questions — "Who am I? What is the meaning of my life? What does my future hold?" — with a certain urgency.

Other transitions are triggered by unforeseen events. I am thinking in a special way of people who have experienced a severe loss: the break-up of a significant relationship, the death of a loved one, unemployment, forced retirement, the loss of deep spiritual beliefs, unrealized potential or simply the absence of reasons for living. I am also thinking of readers who, no longer satisfied with the motivation that kept them going up to this point, are in the midst of an existential crisis; people trapped in a scenario that no longer "fits"; others experiencing continual restlessness or an indefinable boredom. Finally, I am thinking of all those who feel that they have missed the boat in life.

WHAT IS THIS BOOK ABOUT?

Before I wrote this book, five groups of young people and mid-life adults experienced the material contained in it. The meetings were spread out over three weekends. Participants were invited to undertake a three-part spiritual quest: to mourn the past stages of their life, to deepen their identity, and to get a sense of their true mission. At the end of the process, participants agreed almost unanimously that they had acquired greater self-knowledge and a deeper awareness of their mission and of what they wanted to accomplish in life. I now invite you to join this personal quest, which is designed to allow you to discover your mission. The word "quest" comes from the Latin word *quaesitus*, which means both "seeking" and "questioning."

The method outlined here follows roughly the model of change proposed by William Bridges in *Transitions: Making Sense of Life's Changes*. Bridges sees human life as a series of passages or transitions. People must pass through each of these according to a growth pattern that involves three phases: the period of separation, in which they let go of what is past; the liminal or transition period, in which they deepen their sense of identity and of mission; and, finally, the period of implementation, in which they implement their mission in their own community.

This three-phase model is a classic one often seen in initiation rites. Similarly, mythological stories are constructed around three stages: the hero (usually male in the Greek and Roman myths) is called forth and departs, withstands severe testing and, finally, makes a glorious comeback. Many healing rituals follow this schema. For example, the dynamic of the Twelve Steps of Alcoholics Anonymous involves letting go of alcohol, going through internal struggle and experiencing healing.

The first three chapters of this book describe mission theoretically, stressing the importance of following our mission. All subsequent chapters are organized according to the Bridges model. Thus, Chapters 4 and 5 examine the stage of "letting go" through grieving and forgiveness, a necessary stage if we are to feel sufficiently free to embark on the quest. Chapters 6 and 7 describe the "in-between" or liminal period, during which there is an opportunity to deepen our identity and gain a better understanding of what life is asking of us. The next three chapters (8, 9 and 10) deal with appropriate strategies to discover our mission. The final two chapters relate to the last stage – realizing our mission concretely, dealing with various forms of resistance to it and creating a support system.

Some chapters have a series of practical exercises at the end. I suggest you keep a special notebook in which you record your responses to the various exercises as you journey through this process. "Journal of My Discoveries about My Mission," located at the end of this book, is a tool to help you compile the results of your personal quest, synthesize your discoveries and articulate the life project that emerges.

PART ONE

Mission: Some General Concepts

Three stone-cutters,
seated around a table in a tavern,
were resting up from their day's work
and having a beer.
The proprietor of the tavern
asked the first man
what he did for a living.
The man answered, "I cut stones."
The second man, of whom the proprietor asked
the same question, replied,
"I'm cutting stones to build a wall."
The third man did not even wait
for the proprietor's question,
so eager was he to declare with pride,
"I am building a cathedral."

CHAPTER I

Defining Personal Mission

MISSION, CALLING, VISION: A QUESTION OF VOCABULARY

T o avoid any ambiguity, I would like to clarify right from the start the meaning that the word "mission" has in this book. It does not have the meaning it takes on in expressions like *diplomatic mission* or *foreign missions,* where it designates a role or a power entrusted to someone by the appropriate authority. Current literature on the theme of mission also uses two other synonyms to describe the same reality: the terms *calling* (or *vocation*) and *vision*. In religious vocabulary, these words represent a supreme being's invitation to follow a particular path. These words will not be used here in that sense, for our context is psycho-spiritual rather than religious.

Here, the term mission refers to an orientation towards some societal action that is inscribed in each person's soul.

Here, the term *mission* refers to an orientation towards some societal action that is inscribed in each person's soul. In other words, it designates our need to find fulfillment in an activity that corresponds to our identity and serves the community.

The terms *mission, calling* and *vision* are used here to express the same reality, even though they refer to various ways of perceiving: through the emotions, through hearing and through seeing. The differences between these words becomes clear from their etymology. *Mission* (from the Latin *missio,* "I send," and *missus,* "sent") evokes a push, an inner emotional surge. *Calling* is another word for vocation (from the Latin *vocatus,* "called"). It relates to auditory perception or, more accurately, to a call that comes from the depth of a person's soul. *Vision* (from the Latin *visio,* "I see" or *visus,* "seen") relates to visual

Personal mission can take several shapes and forms.

perception. This term normally conveys an image in the mind's eye, a creative idea or a plan to be carried out. I use the word mission most frequently; occasionally, I use vision and calling.

How to define personal mission

According to David Spangler in his book *The Call*, there is only one real mission – to love. Who could argue with that? However, while it is true, it seems to me to be too general. Therefore, I have drawn up a list of more concrete forms of mission which, of course, are in the service of love.

Personal mission can take several shapes and forms. To carry it out adequately, it will sometimes be enough to make work-related changes. For instance, you can accomplish the same task in a different context; develop your knowledge and skills through further study or training; change your attitude towards your job; become your own boss by working for yourself; place more emphasis on teamwork; find a new incentive for the work you do.

In certain cases, the mission consists of developing a new attitude: becoming, for example, more creative, more compassionate, more encouraging, less fearful, more willing to take initiative, more committed, more satisfied, more given to expressing gratitude.

At other times, we must go so far as to change careers or jobs if we want to respond to a persistent "soul-call" to, say, go into a service profession, enter politics, work in the field of international co-operation, create a new form of artistic expression or rekindle an earlier passion.

Finally, carrying out our mission may mean choosing a totally new lifestyle: marrying, having a child, moving to the country, becoming a hermit, joining a community or group that wants to share the same values, or finding a new partner whose spiritual ideal corresponds to our own.

How to recognize your personal mission

Your personal mission will show up in many guises: an ideal to pursue, a passion that drives you, an important goal to strive for, a deep and persistent desire, a lasting spiritual inclination, overflowing enthusiasm for a particular kind of activity, and so forth. It is also possible to discover your personal mission by *not* discovering it or by rejecting it. Indeed, you will then be overcome by boredom, regrets, nostalgia, a feeling of emptiness, recurring dreams or haunting reminders. Even undiscovered or denied, your mission remains a beacon shining in the dark.

We often think people choose their mission freely. It would be more accurate to say that the mission chooses the person.

We often think people choose their mission freely. It would be more accurate to say that the mission chooses the person. When we co-operate with it, it becomes our soul wisdom, our travel guide, keeping us from becoming scattered and lost. It encourages us to concentrate our energies. It helps us make good decisions. And, finally, it enables us to discern who our real allies are on our life adventure. More than just another interesting idea encountered along life's path, your personal mission *is* your life path.

How to discover your mission

Many of us expect that our mission will be revealed from heaven by an appearance of God's gnarled finger, accompanied by thunder and lightning, pointing out our route. No doubt there are historical figures who received indisputable signs of their mission. We have only to think of the biblical prophets — Isaiah, Elijah, and Amos, for example — or Joan of Arc, who heard voices enjoining her to go and "save" France.

But personal mission is usually revealed much more discreetly, in unexpected experiences and circumstances. For

We cannot really prepare for our mission. Rather, we are unwittingly being prepared for it.

instance, we rediscover a book we had left untouched in our library for years or by chance get into an engrossing conversation; we register for a course, initially without a lot of interest, or we learn about a training workshop that's being held; we agree to take on a responsibility that at first glance appears to be out of our league; we get sick, have an accident or go through a divorce. We may witness a painful social situation that moves us, shakes us to the depths of our being. Such events can conspire to compel people to change direction.

Our mission can also come on the scene not through external signs, but through a frame of mind that we tend to ignore or even be unaware of: persistent ruminations, an aversion to specific kinds of work, silent attacks of conscience, flights of fancy, daydreams, an untiring interest, and so forth. The day we finally stop and connect all these subtle inner workings and decipher these multiple signals – which is a bit like blindly following a thread through the maze of our life's events – we will find ourselves face to face with our mission.

Sometimes the deep orientation of our soul announces its presence in a more convincing manner, in the form of a clear call, a disturbing emotion, a sudden inspiration, an irresistible idea, a stroke of genius, an undreamed-of opportunity, an unexpected meeting or a challenging social situation.

One thing is certain: we cannot really prepare for our mission. Rather, we are unwittingly being prepared for it – by our sometimes irrational choices, our timid "yes's," illness, burnout, strange events. Only much later, looking back on the unfolding of our lives, can we see that a mysterious design was guiding us. Usually nature does not do things in leaps, but conditions a person to be able to make the major transitions in life. A woman's menstrual periods serve as a kind of preparation for the pains of childbirth; the numerous small goodbyes in life predispose us to accept the great farewell of death. It is the same with a person's mission: when it calls us to a major stretch, it is counting on the many small "yes's" that have paved the way, making our surrender easier.

Mission and identity

The principal factor in discovering our mission is self-knowledge. Whatever form our mission takes, it is rooted in each individual's identity. In his brilliant work, *Callings*, Gregg Levoy expresses the relationship between calling and identity in this way: "Callings [...] reflect our most fundamental necessities and instincts, the primitive 'I want!' of the soul. By moving against our calls, we move against ourselves. We mistrust our deepest intelligence" (1997:234).

We sometimes hear people say, "My mission in life is just to be." The beauty and candour of this statement do not make it true. Mission flows from being, but is not to be confused with it. The old philosophical adage *"Agere sequitur esse"* [action follows being] still applies today.

In Chapters 6 and 7 we will pursue the theme of identity in greater depth. For now, I simply want to point out that our constant evolution as individuals requires that we ask ourselves, "Who am I?" and revise and update our answer periodically. Especially during times of transition, it is essential that we withdraw from our usual activities to enter into ourselves and reflect on our soul's dream. These times are even more crucial when we have the impression that we are stagnating and just marking time. A river's current seems to disappear when the river flows into a lake, but the current remains active. Likewise, the work of our mission continues even if we sometimes need to interrupt our search to meditate more deeply on our inner being.

Whatever form our mission takes, it is rooted in each individual's identity.

You will be haunted by your mission as by a phantom until you obey it.

Every person's identity is specific, unchangeable and unique; the same is true of our mission in the world. Victor Frankl affirmed this clearly: "We each have our own calling or specific mission in life, one that is unique and cannot be carried out by anyone else, for our life can never be replicated. Each person's task is unique, in that only they can realize this unique opportunity."

THE CHARACTERISTICS OF PERSONAL MISSION

Your mission is inescapable

You cannot escape your mission. Even when the river widens, narrows, is diverted, meanders, threatens to disappear in the swamps or leaps about on the rocks, it is still the same river. That is how it is with your mission. You can flee from it, misinterpret its nature, believe you have found it because you have become popular, or fragment it into myriad activities. Whatever substitute you invent to evade it, whatever pretexts you invoke to delay accomplishing it, you will be haunted by your mission as by a phantom until you obey it.

There is something permanent about your mission. Its essence cannot be transformed over the course of a lifetime, although it can become more defined, concrete and expanded, and benefit a greater number of people. World-renowned violinist Yehudi Menuhin was able to say, "Looking back on the sixty years I have lived, I am struck most of all by the straightforwardness of the pattern. Everything that I am, or think, or do, almost everything that has happened to me, seems traceable to its origins with the simple clarity of geometrical proof. It is a curious, even a faintly disconcerting sensation to find oneself fulfilling what seems to have been a destiny" (1976:3).

In other words, when you stay in touch with your mission, it becomes a beacon in your life, your soul-wisdom, enabling you to make good decisions, choose true friends and engage in activities that offer fulfillment.

No one else can reveal your mission to you. Only you can discover it.

You discover your mission, you don't invent it

Our task is not to create our mission, but to let it find a home in us. In fact, Victor Frankl states that, far from being something we invent, our mission in life is something we can only discover. He describes it as "a monitor or an inner sense, a conscience making us aware of our own uniqueness." It buds forth like a flower, emerging from within us (or, rather, from the Self, as we shall see later on). It lets itself be discerned only gradually. It rarely explodes, but develops slowly, in a way that parallels human growth.

Swiss psychoanalyst Carl Jung said it was impossible to escape from his mission. He felt he was grappling with a *daimon* (the Greek term equivalent to the Latin *genius*, from a verb meaning "to generate/beget/create/give life") that pushed him to act: "There was a *daimon* in me, and in the end its presence proved decisive. It overpowered me, and if I was at times ruthless it was because I was in the grip of the *daimon*. I could never stop at anything once attained. I had to hasten on, to catch up with my vision" (1989:356).

Only you can discover your mission

No one else can reveal your mission to you. Only you can discover it. How we would love someone to reassure us about our calling! Our hope that some wise person will instruct us about exactly what to do in life surprises us. We think it would be so easy if our parents would mark out the path to follow, if a spiritual guide would reveal God's will for us, if a

It is the fruit of your own labour, a labour of reflection and solitude as well as the fear of making mistakes.

psychologist, using the magic of psychological testing, would tell us what direction to take, if a sudden inspiration would come and take away all our hesitations. Alas! You don't discover your mission this way. Rather, it is the fruit of your own labour, a labour of reflection and solitude as well as the fear of making mistakes. Mother Teresa did not let herself get discouraged as she pursued her mission to aid the dying in Calcutta. For seven years, her spiritual director advised her against leaving her community. Nonetheless she persevered and followed her path. How fortunate are those who along the way meet a wise person who can support them in their search and confirm their intuitions regarding their mission.

Who is the author of our mission?

"We begin to realize that our deepest nature, the centre of ourselves, or God within is the *source* of our callings," writes Gregg Levoy in *Callings* (1997:324). This coincides with the thought of Carl Jung, who defined the Self, at the heart of our personality, as the reflection of God in us (the *Imago Dei*). For Jung, the Self is the organizing principle of the whole personality; it is non-temporal, both young and old at the same time; it unites all the traits of the masculine and the feminine; it presides over the healing of our being; finally, the Self knows our mission.

In his book *The Sense of Vocation: A Study of Career and Life Development*, Larry Cochran notes that when his research subjects described their calling, they used — even in a secular context — terms that have a religious connotation: devotion, sacredness, purity, holiness, total commitment of the heart, and so on. The same author compares the experiences of discovering our mission with psycho-spiritual peak experiences (1990:2).

If God were a tyrant or dictator who imposes his will – the image often presented – we would hardly be able to realize our mission in complete freedom. But if, on the other hand, our human talents, aptitudes, deep desires and free impulses express God's will, we shall enjoy a mysterious collaboration with the divine will in carrying out our mission. In this regard, Simone Pacot writes in *L'évangélisation des profondeurs* [Evangelizing from the depths] that doing God's will is each individual's personal response to God's design. Because each human being is unique, each one manifests and embodies God's design in a very specific way, in harmony with who they are (see 1997:143).

Becoming aware that we have a mission to accomplish is simultaneously fascinating and frightening.

Your mission attracts and frightens you at the same time

You won't need to spend a lot of time wondering what you are experiencing when you feel overcome by a persistent inclination, a recurrent interest, a stubborn fascination with a lifestyle or a particular activity. This kind of attraction undoubtedly points to a mission and its profile. Astonishingly, the attraction we feel is often accompanied by great apprehension. Becoming aware that we have a mission to accomplish is simultaneously fascinating and frightening.

A 55-year-old woman who wanted to do studies in pastoral counselling asked me if it was normal at her age to harbour such an ambition. Ever since she began to pursue this project, she felt herself oscillating between enthusiasm and fear. I pointed out to her that her feeling of ambivalence, the mixture of enthusiasm and anxiety, confirmed the authenticity of her project. This feeling highlighted the sacred character of her intent. Anthropologist Rudolf Otto in fact defined the sacred in terms of alternating between fascination and terror (*fascinosum* and *tremendum*).

Seeking your mission requires a serious commitment that cannot be separated from those detachments that we used to call sacrifices.

Your mission demands total commitment

When some young people asked anthropologist and mythologist Joseph Campbell what direction they should take in life, he replied, "Follow your bliss." This succinct piece of advice outlines an entire program for life. At first glance, it could lead you to believe, wrongly, that life would evolve thereafter in a state of pure felicity. However, this is not Campbell's view; he insists instead that you must have the courage to pursue to the end where your happiness takes you. Seeking your mission requires a serious commitment that cannot be separated from those detachments that we used to call sacrifices. These detachments have nothing to do with masochism; they let us renounce something good to choose a greater good, such as self-fulfillment or the realization of our mission.

I myself have experienced that accomplishing our mission requires total commitment. When, at the age of 42, I expressed my desire to pursue studies in psychology, my religious superiors wanted to test the seriousness of my decision and my commitment. The call I felt became increasingly clear and pressing: I spent the better part of my leisure time reading in the field, participating in therapy training sessions and meeting with people who were looking for counselling.

At first I met with opposition from my superiors, who did not believe in my professional development project. Then I risked taking a very expensive trip to San Francisco for a half-hour interview without knowing whether I would be accepted at the university. Once admitted to the program I had chosen, I looked for accommodation in one of the houses of my religious community or in a rectory, as my superiors had required. But nowhere was there room for me. So I went to live on campus with students who were very wary of any adults who mixed with them. I found out in the first few days that my grasp of English was totally inadequate. In addition, I had the problem of finding a placement for a practicum. For a whole semester, I travelled more than 200 kilometres twice a week to get to the placement I had finally found. I won't mention the numerous other hardships I had to endure to realize my dream.

On more than one occasion I was overcome by doubt: "Have I gotten in over my head?" Thanks to my walks along the ocean, I managed to make it through the first semester. During the second semester, to my great astonishment, all the doors seemed to open: my English had improved; a practicum placement became available right near the university; I developed some marvellous friendships; some wonderful families offered me hospitality; I was benefiting enormously from my courses. Even my superiors were reconciled to my study project. I understood then that, when we believe in something, we often have to pass through the impossible to arrive at the possible.

Your mission reaches out to others

The more we learn to love ourselves, the more we learn to love others. This paradox always amazes me. Realizing our calling also has something paradoxical about it. As we find our own mission and live it to the full, we serve the community. We don't apply our talents in isolation: therefore, others must benefit from them. The creative spirit that accompanies the realization of our mission stirs those around us. The poet Kabir wrote, "When a flower opens, the bees are attracted." There is nothing more energizing than the sight of a person in the process of actualizing their resources.

William James also reminds us of the social influence of our inner state on the outer world. He says that the great

As we find our own mission and live it to the full, we serve the community.

Human beings can transform the externals of their lives.

revolution of his generation was the discovery that human beings, by altering their inner mental attitude, can transform the externals of their lives. Thus, discovering our mission and the way we apply ourselves to realizing it will have a mysterious and unforeseeable ripple effect on our entire life and, subsequently, on all our surroundings.

The little boy looked at the star
and began to cry.
The star asked him, "Why are you crying?"
The boy answered, "You are too far away.
I shall never be able to reach you!"
And the star replied,
"O little one, if I were not already in your heart,
you would not be able to see me!"

— JOHN MAGLIOLA

CHAPTER 2

The Importance of Discovering Your Mission

Each time we ask people about their mission, we enter into a mysterious reality that cannot adequately be explained by reason. Indeed, how can we know exactly what the experience was of those who carried out their mission and of those who, on the other hand, rejected it? We will look first at those who said "yes" to the call of their soul, their modes of consent and the consequences. In the next chapter, we will focus on those who were unable or unwilling to follow their mission.

A lot of people seem to have discovered their mission very early — in childhood or adolescence.

ADOLESCENCE AND MID-LIFE: THE MOST FAVOURABLE TIMES TO DISCOVER YOUR MISSION

A lot of people seem to have discovered their mission very early — in childhood or adolescence. I have met priests and religious who, from the age of seven or eight, were sure of their vocation. I have also known educators whose childhood games prefigured their careers as professors or teachers. People who have both a talent and a passion for a particular thing find that this talent and passion indicate their mission, like a destiny to be followed. Think of Mozart and all those young musicians predestined for their art by their precocious musical talent.

There are two specific periods in life when the need to fulfill your mission becomes more imperative and even obsessive: adolescence and mid-life.

Most adolescents remain haunted by the revelation of their profound nature and of the possibilities of their mission.

The intuitions of adolescence

Adolescence is a period fertile with intuition about our life project. In this vein, Robert Johnson, in his book *He: Understanding Masculine Psychology*, tells the story of the fisher-king to illustrate the decisive event he experienced in adolescence. Lost in the forest and starving, the king spotted a salmon being cooked over some hot coals. In trying to take it, he burned his fingers and instinctively brought them to his mouth; in doing so, he tasted a morsel of the fish. This adventure so transformed him that he was never the same again. Johnson saw in this story the drama of the male adolescent who gets a premature "taste" of the essence of his being, with the salmon representing the Self. The disturbing revelation of his identity turns out to be an experience which, by virtue of his young age, the adolescent is unable to accept.

Johnson applies the phenomenon of this symbolic burn to most adolescents; they all remain haunted by the revelation of their profound nature and of the possibilities of their mission. This happens to young people who, in a fleeting moment, glimpse their spiritual essence and their future. During a meeting I attended once, a group of young people were discussing their intuitions about their calling. Several of them acknowledged that they had had peak experiences that had allowed them to glimpse their future.

Unfortunately, most people forget about or ignore these intuitions, these mystical flashes of their future perceived in adolescence. When they reach adulthood, they allow the concerns and demands of societal life to take over: they keep up on topics they feel obliged to be informed about, but in which they have very little interest; they become competitive; they earn their living and support their family, have a social role, accumulate money, seek a prestigious post. They let themselves be weighed down by occupations that have nothing in common with the deep desire of their souls.

I agree with the French writer and filmmaker Jean Cocteau when he says, "The older I get, the more I see that what does not get old is our dreams." To this I would add that it is the dreams of our youth in particular that do not get old.

Mid-life crisis

Mid-life represents another favoured period for becoming aware of our mission. To describe the situation of those who have reached this stage of their existence, Joseph Campbell uses the following analogy: "The first thirty-five or forty years of our life are spent in the effort of climbing a tall ladder to get to the top of a building; when we finally get there, we realize we leaned the ladder against the wrong building."

At mid-life, we tend to take stock of our accomplishments.

At mid-life, we move to the other slope of our existence; it is a time when we tend to take stock of our accomplishments. We think we're somebody because we've made our mark in society. We remember what we have achieved, our past loves, our joys and sorrows, our successes and failures, our realized hopes and our broken dreams. But few people feel fully satisfied with what they see. Most people note their unrealized dreams, unachieved ideals and dashed hopes. The spectre of death often exacerbates the feeling of having fallen short of their ideal in life. Panic-stricken, many try to recreate a new period of youth; they try to start all over. Some will end their marriage to choose a younger spouse; others will adopt a new lifestyle or change careers. Haunted by a sense of not having fulfilled their mission, many feel driven to make numerous changes in their lives. But often they misinterpret what needs to be changed.

Adults in mid-life should begin by delving deep within themselves.

They are content to modify external things instead of asking themselves the fundamental questions: "Who am I? What is the dream of my life? How do I want to spend the time I have left to live?"

Instead of succumbing to the temptation of repeating the exploits of youth, adults in mid-life should begin by delving deep within themselves. In fact, the challenge for people at that age is to explore their latent shadow world, the universe of possibilities that they repressed in their unconscious for fear of being rejected.

After a few sessions of psychotherapy, a middle-aged man came to the conclusion that to feel fulfilled, he needed to take a mistress. His therapist, who couldn't make much sense of the man's reasoning, believed he might be on the wrong track, so she came to consult me. I saw it as a classic case of someone seeking to fill an inner void by external means. This man needed to learn to develop his feminine qualities, which he had ignored up to that point. By reintegrating his feminine "shadow," he would be better able to tune into his emotions and sensitivity and thus discover what he wanted from life. (Chapter 6 will deal in greater depth with the concept of the shadow and its reintegration.)

No age limit for becoming aware of your mission

Sometimes people wonder whether there is an age limit for fulfilling your mission. Definitely not! Seeds that were several thousand years old, found in ancient pyramids, were still successfully sprouted! It is never too late to start realizing your mission. The abundance of resources and leisure time offered by our society gives us an almost limitless range of choices. Thousands of retired people who still enjoy excellent health can benefit from this today. They have a unique opportunity to make up for time stolen from the realization of their mission. Will they know how to take advantage of their retirement and blossom in it, or will they just seek diversion to escape depression and the prospect of death?

If you carry out your mission, you can be sure to find meaning in life.

MISSION: SOURCE OF PERSONAL GROWTH
Your mission gives your life meaning

If you carry out your mission, you can be sure to find meaning in life. You will discover what your soul longs for, and the reason for your existence. You will feel that you are being yourself, that you are experiencing the profound oneness of your being, and that you are leading an authentic life. Finally, you will have the satisfaction of being a salutary influence on those around you.

An existence marked by such a sense of fullness stands in sharp contrast to the existential void affecting many of our contemporaries. Victor Frankl referred to this malaise of the soul as an "existential vacuum" or "existential frustration." It is the psychological pain of those who have neither found a meaning for nor given a meaning to their lives. They react to this inner emptiness in various ways: some declare life to be absurd and contemplate suicide as the way out of their distress; others are determined to fill the void of their existence with all sorts of substitutes, such as alcohol, drugs, gambling, erotic activities or frenetic diversion. There are also those who take refuge in activism to escape the hypnotic effect of silence and solitude. According to the French writer Simone Weil, these are all suicidal behaviours: "If the purpose of your existence is to escape life, you are actually seeking death."

The most visible psychological effect of this existential void is a relentless boredom, a kind of soul fever that translates as unrealized spiritual and psychological potential.

People who have discovered their mission find that it provides them with reasons for living and for being happy, whatever obstacles, problems or suffering they may encounter.

This boredom afflicts not only the emotions but the whole person. Even the cells of the body are bored, as they experience the repercussions of the soul's lethargy. Statistics reveal that many heart attacks take place on Monday morning when people go back to work. The discontent felt by some employees who carry the weight of their job like a millstone around their neck might explain this phenomenon.

On the other hand, people who have discovered their mission find that it provides them with reasons for living and for being happy, whatever obstacles, problems or suffering they may encounter. Victor Frankl liked to quote these words of Nietzsche: "He who has a *why* to live for can bear with almost any *how*" (1965:121). Frankl himself knew how true this declaration was: to survive the atrocities of the concentration camps, he constantly had to find a reason to live.

Pursuing your mission engenders soul-wisdom

Discovering your calling focuses all the aspects of your life. Your mission becomes soul-wisdom that teaches you to reject whatever distracts you from your life project and how to tap into your energies and resources to follow this project. Specifically, it tunes out distractions, resists the temptation to seek immediate satisfaction, rejects useless diversions and the scattering of energy, and ignores detractors and false prophets. In short, it eliminates everything that could stand in the way of your total fulfillment.

It is easy to recognize people who are not living according to their mission: they have a finger in every pie; they do not distinguish between what is essential and what is secondary; they dissipate their efforts in frenetic activism. Like the fly in La Fontaine's fable, they believe they are the only ones who make a difference and blame others for not acting. Moreover, they make themselves easy prey for those in search of volunteers. In the end, they suffer from burnout, for they failed to learn earlier on how to listen to and follow their deepest aspirations. Those who do not trust the direction of their mission can expect disaster. (The etymology of the word "disaster" is revealing: *dis-aster* refers to deviating from your star and, hence, getting lost.)

When we suffer from poor self-esteem we do not dare expose ourselves to failure, ridicule, disappointment, criticism.

Realizing your mission: an antidote to lack of self-esteem

Self-esteem, a psychological reality that is under much discussion today, is composed of two different aspects. The first is esteem for your being; the second is confidence in your actions. This simple distinction would help end the war that self-esteem theorists engage in. For some of them, self-esteem is "feeling good" while for others, it is the ability to produce and to create. The first definition is situated in the order of *being*, the second in the order of *doing*. Mission, as I use the term here, relates mainly to self-esteem in the order of doing.

In her book *Le Soi* [The Self], Delphine Martinot notes that poor self-esteem prevents us from taking calculated risks. When we suffer from poor self-esteem we do not dare expose ourselves to failure, ridicule, disappointment, criticism. We would rather disappear from the face of the earth. And yet the most comforting thing for a fragile self that is afraid to fail would be to discover its mission and commit to it. The tiniest success in realizing our mission is a tonic for our self-esteem and encourages us to take further initiatives. Gradually the fear of taking risks disappears and gives way to self-confidence.

Psychology recognizes that the primordial factor needed to persevere in accomplishing a task is self-confidence, which is acquired and maintained through the hope of success. Self-

Self-esteem and mission are intimately linked with and influence each other.

confidence and self-realization through your mission mutually reinforce each other. Their interaction confers the courage and boldness you need to commit to and persevere in your mission.

Self-esteem and mission are therefore intimately linked with and influence each other: the more self-confidence you have, the more you will persevere in realizing a project or a career, because you feel you are being fulfilled. The more committed you feel to your life project, the more self-confident you are, the more motivated you feel to follow your initiatives through to the end.

When I taught high school, I was always amazed at how the academically weak students blossomed in extra-curricular activities. While unable to concentrate on school subjects, they could spend hours collecting stamps, reading complicated mechanics manuals, learning the names of athletes and their achievements in the world of sports, and so on. By enthusiastically carrying out these activities, these students were fostering their own self-esteem.

High school "dropouts" are young people who are discouraged because they have not found an interesting goal in life. It is important to help them discover their mission. This would enable them to develop self-confidence and, consequently, to persevere in their studies.

Being seriously committed to your mission brings support from the universe and its resources

Albert Einstein believed that the fundamental question to be asked in life was this: "Is the universe a friendly place?" In my view, the following story illustrates that if you take your mission seriously, you will find that the universe is friendly and people around you are co-operative.

A friend of mine named Fred had always felt powerfully drawn to people going through bereavement. Should he give up his career as an educator in psychology, which guaranteed him financial security? Should he risk a huge drop in income and start doing psychotherapy with people who find themselves in mourning? Just thinking about changing jobs almost sent him into a panic. Would he be able to earn a living and support his family? Was this some far-fetched idea, a passing whim? What would other people say? Would he regret it for the rest of his life?

After long and anguished hesitation and after consulting with his family and a few friends, Fred took the plunge.

Finally, after long and anguished hesitation and after consulting with his family and a few friends, Fred took the plunge. He resigned from his teaching position and, after training in grief therapy, offered his services to his community. After a slow start, he eventually built up a solid clientele. Then he began to lecture on the subject. It was not long before he acquired an international reputation for his training sessions for grief counsellors. He developed new techniques for grief therapy that he anticipates describing in an upcoming book. His "yes" to his mission propelled him into a series of happy adventures and exciting projects. The reality exceeded his wildest dreams. Because he committed himself deeply to a field he was passionate about, the friendly universe came to meet him.

By contrast, many people consider the universe a threatening reality from which they need to protect themselves. They isolate themselves and refuse to trust; they erect barriers and avoid risks. This increasingly popular way of life, called "cocooning," where each of us is closed off in our well-protected, cozy little world, effectively rules out the beautiful notion of risk-taking.

Every time a person develops their talents and originality in the free accomplishment of their mission, they join as co-creators and collaborators in the work of creation.

Accomplishing your mission enriches the universe

The great eco-theologian Thomas Berry defines three principles that govern the universe: differentiation, interiority, and communion. For billions of years, the universe has been expanding its wealth through the diversification of matter and, for millions of years, through the diversification of earth's plant and animal species. Likewise, every human being is called to become different and unique but, while plants and animals can simply rely on natural laws and instinct to become differentiated, we need to use our free will and our creativity to do so. Thus, every time a person develops their talents and originality in the free accomplishment of their mission, they join as co-creators and collaborators in the work of creation. They enrich the world by their unique and irreplaceable contribution. For the saying "No one is indispensable" we should substitute "Everyone is indispensable." Every human being in fact receives a call to accomplish a personal mission that only he or she can fulfill. If the universe is diminished by the loss of a plant or an animal species, it is just as diminished when individuals do not recognize their mission or refuse to fulfill it.

✝ ✝ ✝

Here in a few words is the essence of these preliminary reflections on the importance of following your life project.

- We sense the call of mission most strongly in two periods of life: adolescence and mid-life.

- There is no age limit for accomplishing your mission, as it is an inborn reality waiting to be explored.

- Pursuing your mission provides a reason for living and gives life meaning.

- Discovering your mission increases your self-esteem and self-confidence.

- The impact of your life project is much wider than you can imagine. By realizing your mission, you are connecting yourself to "energy fields" in the universe.

- By following the call that comes from the depths of your being, you enter into the movement of co-creating the universe. You participate in a universal intelligence and wisdom called Providence.

Pursuing your mission provides a reason for living and gives life meaning.

"My heart is afraid that it will have to suffer,"
the boy told the alchemist
one night as they looked up at the moonless sky.

"Tell your heart that the fear of suffering
is worse than the suffering itself.
And that no heart has ever suffered
when it goes in search of its dreams."

— PAULO COELHO,
THE ALCHEMIST

CHAPTER 3

Those Who Refuse Their Mission

How is it that some people discover their mission and others never do? This remains a mystery. In this chapter we will examine the obstacles we may encounter during the process of discovering our mission.

People who are unaware that their mission exists experience a vague uneasiness that sometimes turns into anxiety attacks and depression.

THOSE WHO HAVE NOT DISCOVERED THEIR MISSION

Those who have not discovered their mission can be described in five categories:

1) those who do not know they have a mission or who do not believe in such a reality;
2) those who seek their mission in vain because they don't know how to look for it;
3) those who do not have the courage to follow it and get by with making compromises;
4) those who found their mission but then abandoned it; and
5) those who have discovered their mission but refuse outright to obey it.

In the first category, we find people who are unaware that their mission exists. Their life evolves dispassionately; the daily routine of eat-work-sleep seems to satisfy them. However, their mission, even if unrecognized, continues to haunt them in the form of fleeting but insistent fantasies. They experience a vague uneasiness that sometimes turns into anxiety attacks and depression. Some tell themselves, "That's

Whenever I talk on the theme of personal mission, I am always amazed to see how the faces of my listeners light up.

all there is to life!" They have repressed their mission deep into their subconscious to the point where it will henceforth be part of their shadow.

Whenever I talk on the theme of personal mission, I am always amazed to see how the faces of my listeners light up in response to this topic; it sparks their interest and fills them with enthusiasm. I get the sense that I am revealing to them an intimate secret that has been kept well hidden in the bottom of their hearts. A young man confided to me recently, "Your talk on how each of us carries within us a mission has changed my life. I just had to tell you."

The second category corresponds to people who run into problems discovering and pursuing their mission. I refer to these obstacles throughout my book, especially in the last part of this chapter. If you would like to read more about kinds of resistance, I recommend Barbara Sher's book *I Could Do Anything If I Only Knew What It Was*, which offers practical strategies for overcoming resistance.

Instead of living their mission, people in the third category are satisfied with compromise. For instance, someone called to be an artist will become an art critic. A potential historian is content to become a general journalist. Someone else, haunted by the need to write, goes into publishing. The single person who would like to have children teaches other people's children. Some try to accomplish their mission in a vicarious manner by choosing a spouse who will do it for them — like the woman who had obvious artistic talent and married an artist. Once she became aware of her unconscious motive, she started to take courses in painting — to her husband's great confusion. He thought she no longer loved him!

In my workshops on discovering your mission, I meet people who at first had found their mission but then had abandoned it. These people fit into the fourth category. Here are a few examples. While working on the outline of her mission, a young woman realized that she had given up work that actually gave her a lot of happiness. As a freelancer, she had created study programs that she tried out with children, whose company she adored. Now, from behind the four walls of her office, she was carrying out her boss's orders. She hated her job because she was no longer exercising her creativity and missed the children. Another participant was amazed to recognize his mission in work that he had given up ten years earlier; he had been an ecologist who led a team of people in the outdoors. Dissatisfied with his current work, he wondered whether he should not return to his former love, even though it might mean a reduced salary.

History offers us examples of well-known heroes who could be classified in the fifth category, people who refused to respond to their mission. The biblical character of Jonah is the typical reluctant prophet who tries to sidestep his calling. God asks him to go and preach to the inhabitants of Nineveh to convert them. Jonah thinks he can escape in a boat headed for Tarsus, in the opposite direction from the location of his mission. However, a great storm starts up at sea. Jonah consents to the crew throwing him overboard to win the favour of the gods in the hope they will calm the waves. A huge fish swallows him up, keeping him prisoner in its stomach. It regurgitates him later…on the banks of the Tigris, in Nineveh. In spite of himself, Jonah finds himself in the very spot where God had asked him to go. The moral of this story is that we do not escape our

In my workshops on discovering your mission, I meet people who at first had found their mission but then had abandoned it.

We do not escape our mission. Either we accomplish it voluntarily or we are led to it by force.

mission. Either we accomplish it voluntarily or we are led to it by force.

A Latin proverb describes the imperative character of mission: "Destiny guides those who accept her. Those who oppose her she takes by force." On the other hand, the option of not obeying our mission is proof of our personal freedom. Our calling is not some implacable fate, as the Greek tragedies would have us believe. We can always rebel against our mission. But if we do, we will pay the price.

What God whispers to the rose
to make it blossom in all its beauty,
God has cried out a thousand times in my heart.

RUMI

REAL OBSTACLES, FALSE BELIEFS AND WAYS OF RESISTING YOUR MISSION

You may encounter three types of obstacles in the pursuit of your mission: real problems, false beliefs and psychological resistance.

Real problems

Not all obstacles are imaginary, and failing to overcome them is not necessarily a sign of a lack of courage. Some very real obstacles may, at least temporarily, thwart the pursuit of your mission: poverty, illness, family responsibilities, lack of resources, isolation, lack of adequate training, and so forth.

These limitations are real. However, we should not underestimate how creative, tenacious and ingenious people can be when they have decided to carry out, at all costs, the dream in their soul. A good case in point is the story of

Marlene. Abandoned by an alcoholic husband, she managed to survive with her two children despite great poverty. I have to admit that when I learned that she was registering in the Master's program in counselling, I did not see how she could succeed. I was wrong. Thanks to her resourcefulness, determination, freelance work and some study bursaries, she succeeded and, after five years, obtained the university degree she wanted. She then set up a practice. It is noteworthy that, given her own experience of poverty, she was very sensitive to her clients who had experienced the same destitution.

You may encounter three types of obstacles in the pursuit of your mission: real problems, false beliefs and psychological resistance.

False beliefs

The second type of obstacle to fulfilling one's mission arises when we take a conviction to be an irrefutable truth when it is not. These erroneous opinions stem from repeated experiences, often unhappy ones. Let me describe a few such opinions here and show why they are false.

My job, my role, or my career: that is my mission!

How fortunate are those whose mission is expressed in their work. But it is particularly important not to confuse these two realities. Jobs, roles and even careers often lack the characteristics of a mission, especially its all-pervasive, permanent and entrancing character. They are subject to change. You can lose your job or abandon one career for another without any change in the emphasis of your personal mission. If you compare the realization of mission to the performance of a piece of music, the mission could be identified with the melody, while the job, role or career could be likened to the instruments. Despite the diversity of the instruments, the melody is always the same.

It is impossible to imitate another person's mission as such.

If you are not so fortunate as to have your work and your mission coincide, your work will not easily provide you with a reason for living; at best, it will give you a reason to survive. Some people in this situation choose a hobby that corresponds more closely to their calling. For example, one of my physician friends found that making and restoring antique furniture has allowed him to express a long-standing personal passion.

I can accomplish my mission by imitating the mission of a great figure

While we can imitate the courage and determination another person showed in the discovery and pursuit of his or her mission, it is impossible to imitate another person's mission as such. The following lines, taken from the Bhagavad Gita, an important sacred text in Hindu philosophy, stress this point: "It is better to do your own duty [dharma], however imperfectly, than to assume the duties of another person, however successfully" (1954:48).

I witnessed an example of this kind of mistaken thinking when Eugene de Mazenod, founder of my religious order, the Oblates, was made a saint. At that time, much emphasis was placed on his charism, and some members of the order presented it as a quality to be emulated. I thought this was wrong because, besides being unable to imitate such an eminent figure, one person could not hope to exercise another person's charism without deceiving themselves. They risk creating a double personality. Bishop de Mazenod's courage and perseverance in faithfulness to his calling no doubt serve as a great source of inspiration, but no one in a religious order can aspire to live out exactly the founder's charism. Each person will have to discover for himself his own particular gift or "charism."

The more you fulfill your mission, the more you feel independent, creative and in charge of your life. Laurie Beth Jones tells us, "You are either living your mission, or you are living someone else's" (1996:xviii).

If I carry out my superior's wishes, I can't go wrong regarding my mission

Sometimes obedience to our superior or our boss can turn out to be a subtle trap that distracts us from our mission. In fact, it is quite rare to find people in authority whose primary interest is to foster the fulfillment of their subordinates or employees in the realization of their life project. On the contrary, they are more concerned with running the institution or the company for which they are responsible. Employees can become victims of the short-term vision of their bosses and often end up working for motives that are unrelated to the fulfillment of their mission: a good salary, fringe benefits or a promotion. When this happens, they do not have a sense of realizing their full potential. Estelle Morin, in her article "L'efficacité organisationelle et le sens du travail" ["Organizational efficiency and the meaning of work"], published in the anthology *La quête du sens* [The search for meaning] (Pauchant, 1996), concluded that, currently, this is the main reason for the tensions, absenteeism, sabotage and exaggerated demands in the world of work.

Young people will feel the need to accomplish their mission less urgently than adults. Generally young people need to delay the realization of their mission in order to carry out more immediate responsibilities, such as supporting themselves and carving out a place for themselves in life. They must adapt to the available work possibilities and to the circumstances of their lives. But

Young people will feel the need to accomplish their mission less urgently than adults.

49

I have met people who were depressed because they pursued an ideal dictated by an institution.

when people reach mid-life, the need to realize the mission for which they came into the world becomes more pressing.

As a psychologist, I have met people who were depressed because they pursued an ideal dictated by an institution, an ideal that had nothing to do with their personal aspirations. On this point, Laurie Beth Jones warns her readers in *The Path: Creating Your Mission Statement for Work and for Life*, "Beware of taking on missions that fit someone else's needs – but not your particular interests or gifts" (1996:16). It is not surprising that many workers have but one goal in life: to reach retirement age, when they will finally be free of the demands of a job that does not correspond to their mission.

The leaders of some institutions are convinced that, if members apply themselves to fulfilling the institution's mission, they will no longer need to seek their own. Here is an eloquent illustration of this phenomenon. Each year some religious were required to make a retreat to rekindle their apostolic and spiritual vigour. Year after year, a new speaker was brought in to present the general mission of the Church. Curiously, despite the competence of these speakers, the retreatants hardly appreciated their remarks. But one day, a new speaker-facilitator evoked great enthusiasm in his listeners. He started off by inviting them to ask themselves about their personal mission. Once they had identified it, he then encouraged them to situate it within a specific niche of the Church's mission.

This facilitator had understood, on the one hand, the primary need to respect the call of each individual and, on the other hand, the possibilities within the apostolic mission of the Church to accommodate individual gifts or charisms.

I can discover my life mission by studying philosophy or theology

Seeking and discovering your mission lie beyond purely intellectual analysis. Some people believe that studying the great philosophical and theological systems will help them to identify their deep aspirations. Certainly, this type of study may be useful in helping them find the meaning of life, but not the meaning of their own life. In fact, there is a huge difference between philosophizing about the meaning of life in general and finding the meaning of one's own life, which is embodied in a personal mission. No philosophical study will replace the need to "know thyself" and, consequently, the need to reflect on personal identity and mission.

Seeking and discovering your mission lie beyond purely intellectual analysis.

When I am well known, that will be the sign that I have achieved my mission

Fame in itself has nothing to do with the true nature of our mission. Certainly, social recognition of our mission by a group is necessary. But popularity and honours are incidental to personal mission. Its authenticity is determined by inner criteria: enthusiasm, creativity and the satisfaction of making a unique contribution to the world.

I know performing stars who are unhappy and dissatisfied with themselves and I know workers who feel totally fulfilled. I think of a gardener who loved his plants and flowers and took great pride in the order and beauty of his flower beds. He always had a friendly greeting for the passersby who came to watch him work. Judging from the ardour he brought to his task, the attention he gave it and his continual good humour, here was a man whose happiness derived from the fulfillment of his mission.

Each of us enjoys the full freedom to adopt the path that is in keeping with our authentic self.

Whatever I do in life, I am the plaything of fate or of a blind destiny

Someone defined fate as the name God uses when travelling incognito. Without dwelling on the mystery of coincidence or predestination, I want to state my conviction that, despite the risks in life, we are free to choose our mission. We are not the puppets of destiny. On the contrary, each of us enjoys the full freedom to adopt the path that is in keeping with our authentic self. Animals are fulfilled by virtue of their programmed instincts; humans, however, are fulfilled thanks to their free will. They must also decipher their soul's secret code, their "spiritual DNA" – to use a favourite expression of James Hillman's in *The Soul's Code* – and co-operate with it.

Following your mission is really tough

Pursuing your mission, especially at first, can be a source of real anxiety. After all, you are facing the unknown. We never know what a particular life choice has in store for us: we are afraid of making a mistake; we anticipate failure; we sense the possibility of rejection by family and friends; we might even surprise ourselves by dreading a success that would demand too much of us. On the other hand, once you are keenly committed to your mission, you will see these fears gradually dissipate as they give way to satisfaction and a feeling of inner harmony. You then have the impression of coming home to yourself after a long exile.

The initial fears connected with choosing a new direction in life are often transformed into passionate enthusiasm. However, if fears, anxiety and suffering persist, these should be taken as a sign of being on the wrong track. If, therefore, after a serious effort, you do not feel deep joy in answering a call, you should re-direct your life in another way. The discovery and realization of your mission can only result in joy, happiness, creativity and a desire to live ever more fully.

The desire to be fulfilled through a mission goes hand in hand with loving yourself.

Seeking your mission fosters selfishness

It must be recognized that the desire to be fulfilled through a mission goes hand in hand with loving yourself. It is a paradox that our love of others depends on our love of self. This is the meaning of the gospel precept "You shall love your neighbour as yourself." St. Thomas Aquinas uses this scriptural citation to authorize his teaching that love of self has primacy over love of the other. He taught that because love of self provides the model for love of neighbour, the former ranks ahead of the latter. A person's search for personal mission is inspired by this same logic and has an altruistic dimension, paradoxical as that may seem.

People who are pursuing their mission will note sooner or later its beneficial effects on those around them and on society. Even if our initial motives are tainted with selfishness, gradually these will be purified, especially as we mature. For instance, an industrialist who started out by focusing on amassing a fortune later became the patron of a group of artists; an inventor who started off solely in the spirit of competition ended up making major technological discoveries that benefited humanity; a Latin American priest who was consecrated a bishop mainly because he belonged to his country's aristocracy surprised many people when he sided with the poor.

Besides, the temptation to be selfish is constant in our lives. The experience of easy success may make us believe we are superior and lead to self-glorification and ego inflation. Indeed, as we approach the Self, we will feel enthusiasm (from the Greek word meaning "inhabited by God") and be susceptible

As we approach the Self, we will feel enthusiasm and be susceptible to pride.

to pride (the hubris the ancient Greeks warned against). Succumbing to this temptation will make a person conceited and sterile; inspiration and creativity will soon dry up.

My talent is my mission

A young woman confided to me that she had been pressured by her teachers to become a professional pianist because, they would point out, she won every competition she entered. There was no doubt that she loved playing the piano, but it was not her desire to make a career of it; she saw herself, rather, in education. Mistakenly, some reminded her of the parable of the talents to influence her choice of mission. The parable invites us to bring to fruition what the Creator has planted in our hearts – not this or that skill. In fact, the word "talent" in the parable refers to a monetary coin, not an ability.

This young woman went ahead and made a career for herself as a pianist, but she always remained dissatisfied. After hesitating a long time – she did not want to "betray" her talent – she decided to devote herself instead to journeying with terminally ill patients. For the first time, she felt she was following the impulse of her heart. As for her musical talent, she put it at the service of her new-found mission.

Psychological resistance

In addition to actual problems and to the false beliefs that people may hold about mission, psychological resistance constitutes a third type of obstacle. There is a lot of misunderstanding on the subject of resistance and how to deal with it. The most common attitude is reflected in the saying "Where there's a will, there's a way." It implies that if there is enough desire, any obstacle is surmountable and that if people are resisting following their mission, they are either lazy or not serious in their intent.

I believe, however, that resistance comes from an unconscious part of ourselves manifesting its disapproval of the conscious project. If this unconscious part resists, it is because it fears being forgotten or set aside in favour of the central project to be pursued. It is important, therefore, to understand the message that our resistance is conveying: it is warning us that the goal being pursued is not taking into account all our soul's needs and that it is not safeguarding the interests of the whole person.

I will deal at greater length with the problem of the various kinds of psychological resistance in Chapter 11 of this book. However, I would like to insist at this point on the importance of resistance and how we handle it. Resistance plays an essential role both in self-knowledge and in the enlightened and effective search for our mission. Carl Jung warns those who are tempted to get rid of their resistance as if it were a bad tooth: "We would have gained nothing, but would have lost as much as thinkers deprived of their doubt, or moralists deprived of their temptation, or the brave deprived of their fear. This would not be a cure. It would be an amputation" (cited in *Callings*, p. 196).

When clients show strong resistance in psychotherapy, it is an obvious sign that they are touching upon a critical point in their growth. Likewise, fierce resistance to carrying out our mission reveals that we are being called to make a major change in our lives. Despite appearances, resistance is good news: the anxiety we experience indicates that we are approaching something important, even sacred. Therefore, the appropriate way to handle this resistance is to welcome it, let it emerge, name it and make it a potential ally in the discernment and accomplishment of our mission.

I believe that resistance comes from an unconscious part of ourselves manifesting its disapproval of the conscious project.

PART TWO

Letting Go

*A man who wanted to reach the level
of enlightenment decided to place himself
under the guidance of a great spiritual master.
First the master invited him to take tea
with him. The neophyte used the opportunity
to rhyme off his university degrees and to
describe his spiritual experiences.*

*While he was talking, the master continued
to pour him tea, even when the cup
began to overflow. Astonished at this strange gesture,
the future disciple asked him what he was doing.
The master answered, "Do you not see
that there is no room left in you
for my teachings?"*

CHAPTER 4

Saying your goodbyes

Mission and transitions

Mission, calling, vision…these realities all concern a person's future. That future, however, will be impossible to realize unless the person makes use of the present to let go of the past. William Bridges reminds us that it is in fact necessary to break with what has gone before in order to plan the future: "Every transition," he writes, "begins with an ending" (1980:11).

As long as we stubbornly hold on to what no longer is, we are condemned to stay imprisoned there.

As long as we stubbornly hold on to what no longer is, we are condemned to stay imprisoned there, to live in an unreal world and then to stagnate in psychic and spiritual sterility. The way certain people refuse to let go makes you think of the attitude of those monkeys that allow themselves to be captured so easily by aboriginal people. The hunters deposit nuts into small-necked vases which they then disperse throughout the forest. When the monkeys push their paw in to take a fistful of nuts, they cannot get it out because the neck is too narrow. Unless they let go of the nuts, they are trapped by the vase and become easy prey.

Before we can enter a new phase, we must separate from the past by creating changes, not just on the outside, but especially on the inside. Many people do not get beyond the dream stage. Their search for their mission is on hold while they remain the prisoners of unresolved grief, entangled in painful memories. As a result, their plans for the future are paralyzed or seriously impaired. A little string around an eagle's foot is, after all, enough to keep it from spreading its wings to fly up to the mountaintops. Meister Eckhart reminds us, "If you wish to become what you were meant to be, you must cease to be what you are."

To resolve our grief we must become aware of our losses.

If we can manage to let go of what in any event belongs to a bygone era, in other words, die to what is over, an unexpected thing will take place. By renouncing the old, we begin to come alive again and find once more the desire to grow. This is why it is of the greatest importance to say our goodbyes, to let go so we can deepen who we are and then be ready to realize our life project.

To resolve our grief we must become aware of our losses, name them and progress through various stages. I thought it could be useful to draw up a list of the various kinds of losses that we may be liable to experience along life's journey.

THE LOSSES EXPERIENCED ALONG LIFE'S JOURNEY

The foreseeable losses and the necessary acts of renunciation

Every period of life – birth, childhood, adolescence, life as a couple, marriage, mid-life, children leaving home (empty nest), retirement, old age – begins with a separation from the previous stage. It is the inescapable law that one must die to be reborn. Judith Viorst, in her book *Necessary Losses*, describes in detail the separations required by any transition period. Here are a few examples.

Many young people seek their calling but have great difficulty finding it. One of the main reasons for their foundering may well be the lack of any kind of initiation that would have enabled them to sever their family ties. Young men in particular have greater difficulty "cutting the umbilical cord" that connects them to their mothers. Many of them do not evolve and remain in the grip of the *Puer aeternus* (eternal child) archetype. When the time comes to choose a spouse, they seek someone who will continue playing the role of the ideal mother. Generally, girls are more successful at freeing themselves from their families. However, a good many of them stay under the influence of their father's authority for a long time. They are afraid to betray their father by becoming themselves – like the young woman who wanted desperately to become a professional decorator, but stuck with her work as an accountant since she didn't want to risk upsetting her father.

Some transitions can be traumatic.

Some transitions can be traumatic – as in the case of a new mother who feels depressed and does not understand why she does not feel happier about having given birth to a healthy baby. The arrival of her child has turned her life upside down: maternity leave from work, less intimacy with her husband, little time for her leisure pursuits, etc. She thinks she is abnormal and feels she is a bad mother. What is really happening is that she has not yet accepted the renunciation involved in becoming a new mother.

Nor does a happy event like a promotion or a new direction spare us the pangs of separation. A friend of mine who was a school principal finally saw her dream come true: to teach college. And yet, since then, she has felt more uncomfortable than ever. She was surprised at how much she missed the rewarding aspects of her former work.

It is like that for many retired people, too, if they have not said goodbye to their job. Indeed, we sometimes imagine that if we have been looking forward to retirement for a long time, there will be no need to mourn the end of our employment. A teacher I knew awaited with great anticipation the day she could retire. She had prepared meticulously. So she was completely baffled when, at the end of the school year, she could not stop crying as she said

The absolutely essential condition for being able to welcome your new mission is learning to let go of the past.

goodbye to her students and her colleagues. She had assumed that preparing for her retirement guaranteed that she would not feel sad. But her preparation did not exempt her from the renunciation that a transition requires. It did, however, enable her to make that renunciation more peacefully.

What can we say about those who have not thought about negotiating similar passages in their lives? Like the mother who has been depressed ever since her children left home, because she cannot envision what a mother might become without children to look after, they cling desperately to a life scenario they have already outgrown.

Therefore, the absolutely essential condition for being able to welcome your new mission is learning to let go of the past, despite your impression that it will kill you to do so. Richard Bach, author of *Illusions: The Adventures of a Reluctant Messiah*, writes, "What the caterpillar calls the end of the world, the master calls a butterfly" (1998:134).

Unforeseeable losses

In addition to the foreseeable losses in life, there are the unexpected ones: the sudden death of a loved one, an accident, a divorce, being "let go," bankruptcy, failure, disappointment in love, etc. The suddenness and unexpectedness of these losses often make it much more difficult to resolve your grief. Despite the dramatic nature of this type of loss, it is still possible to go through the process of grieving it.

What you need to lose to pursue your ideal

We are afraid of the unknown. Why jeopardize a well-ordered, comfortable life and commit to a mission that might turn out to be a pipe dream? After achieving financial security, an easy life and enviable social status, you are hardly inclined to risk losing everything that guarantees your security. What will win out? Your dreams, which might or might not be successfully realized, or the attitude that "a bird in the hand is worth two in the bush"?

A priest faced the following dilemma. He had successfully set up several useful projects in the community. But these projects did so well that he had been forced to hand over their ownership and management to a company. The company had hired him on as an employee to administer a service division. Gradually, he began to feel unhappy in his new role. He went into a depression and the chest pains he hadn't experienced in some time returned. His work caused him such stress that he had to see a psychotherapist. The therapist advised him to quit the routine job and to use his creativity more, as he had done earlier in responding to urgent social problems. But such a change in calling represented an enormous drop in salary. How would he be able to cover the costs of his new house, his luxury car, his expensive leisure pursuits? Rather than follow his creative talent and adopt a more modest lifestyle, he chose to maintain the status quo and take pills for his angina.

How many people, like him, reject the prospect of a calling that would entail enormous changes to their lifestyle? Many people would rather silence these dreams, which threaten their peace and security. They find excuses and refuse to pay attention to the constant longing in their soul. As a result, they are uneasy: they feel bored, gloomy, aggressive, depressed. The mere thought of compromising what they have acquired paralyses them. Why give up so much material investment, all the human relationships, the comfortable

How many people reject the prospect of a calling that would entail enormous changes to their lifestyle?

When life loses its meaning for us, it manifests itself in the form of melancholy, moodiness or being bored with existence.

habits, a guaranteed retirement, talents well developed through years of practice? Why give up all these tangible benefits to embrace a dream that might never be realized?

Losses that are hard to discern

When life loses its meaning for us, it manifests itself in the form of melancholy, moodiness or being bored with existence. This condition afflicts many people today. The world is colourless, the heart is heavy; feelings of discontent, emptiness and futility take over. Nothing satisfies, nothing excites them. What used to be the joy of their life they no longer find fulfilling. They languish in an existential void that they try to fill with things and activities that only end up making them feel even more disappointed. Some become skeptics, others turn into bullies. Some withdraw into an unhealthy isolation, others take refuge in consumption, illness or depression. Some try to fill the inner void through alcoholism or inappropriate sexual behaviour, if they do not let themselves be tempted by suicidal thoughts: "What's the point of living? Is there nothing more to life than the same old routine? Why keep going?" These are all signs of existential neurosis.

Viktor Frankl defines existential frustration as the radical absence of meaning in a person's life. The root of spiritual neurosis is the absence of a reason for living, especially in a person who has lost all passion. Where can one go to be cured from this gloomy feeling, from being "down in the dumps"? What would give renewed meaning to our life? The answer lies, to a great extent, in the discovery of our mission.

THE STAGES OF LETTING GO

The aim of psychological grief work is not to make us forget, but to establish a new relationship with the realities that have been precious to us, be these people, activities, talents or material things. Remember here the particular nature of the grief process: it is at the same time natural, gradual, community-based and temporary. It is natural because it is set in motion by itself as soon as we stop resisting. It is gradual because grief is resolved in successive stages. It is community-based because we cannot be healed from grief without the help of others, especially the support of a sympathetic community. Finally, it is temporary because, as the grief begins to resolve itself, the grieving person rediscovers a new psychological and spiritual equilibrium.

My experience of accompanying the bereaved has led me to divide the grief process into seven stages.

My experience of accompanying the bereaved has led me to divide the grief process into seven stages. These are really seven reference points that enable a person to recognize how far they have progressed in their grief and to measure how much they have begun to let go. Here is a short description of each of these stages. You will find them presented in greater detail in my book *How to Love Again: Moving from Grief to Growth.*

I. Shock

We normally meet the letting-go phase with great resistance: shock and denial. These stages, however, prove to be beneficial for the bereaved. They give the person the time needed to ease the suffering and build the resources that will make it possible to face the inevitable. In other words, this resistance helps the grieving person to metabolize the suffering bit by bit, thereby avoiding too great a despondency.

Shock is a kind of stupor or even shattering that paralyzes our perception of the harsh reality facing us. Unable to imagine such a loss, we have the impression of

Our mechanisms for resisting grief play a positive role.

living in a bad dream from which we want to be awakened. We are obsessed with memories of the past that drown out the reality of the present. Sometimes we even hallucinate.

2. Denial

Denial is the second reflex defence mechanism against awareness of our loss. It operates in two ways: it makes us forget the painful event and makes us repress the strong emotions of our grief. The first temptation is to go back to the "good old days," to forget the present situation and to believe that everything will once again be like it was before. Alas! Life never repeats itself; it does not permit us to relive the past.

The second temptation is to imagine that it is possible to avoid the work of grieving. We try to replace the loss: we hurry to replace our spouse with another, our job with another, our dog with another dog, and so forth. This is often the case with men. After a divorce or the death of a spouse, men frequently seek out the company of a young woman to fill the inner void and as a balm for their narcissistic wound. This leap forward is deceiving; it makes us believe we have resolved our grief and found a totally new direction in our life. Illusion! It is impossible to evade our grief without paying the price later.

Our mechanisms for resisting grief, then, play a positive role: they give us time to "survive," to digest the loss at a pace we can handle and to gather our forces to face the most difficult moments of separation. But if we persist in this stage, the process of resolving our grief will be paralyzed and our ability to be open to others and to other projects will be impeded. In that case, bereaved people should seek help without delay to enable them to break through their resistance.

3. Expressing emotions

When their resistance to grief starts to give way, the person grieving feels progressively submerged by a flood of emotions and feelings: fear, sadness, aloneness, abandonment, anger, guilt, liberation, and so forth. These waves of emotion rise up in the person, recede and return again, like the ebb and flow of the sea, each time, however, losing some of their intensity.

Expressing emotion is not limited to the loss of someone dear to us.

Expressing emotion is not limited to the loss of someone dear to us. At the news of being laid off, of divorce or even of a promotion, the "mourner" immediately feels overcome by anxiety. The unknown, even in the case of good news, is perceived as a threat. The "mourner" then has the impression of losing control over the direction of his or her life. Think of parents witnessing their children's definitive departure from home. They are sad at the thought of letting their fledglings fly away, leaving them behind in an empty nest.

Sadness, often called "sorrow," is the emotion that characterizes the state of mourning. During that time, the person feels as if they have just had the object of their affections amputated. This kind of pain often plunges a person into depression, if not desolation, like the state of those who would rather die with their loved one than live without them.

The loss of a job, a pet, an ideal or a dream may at first glance seem less tragic than a death or a divorce, but in some cases it is no easier to bear. I remember the situation of a librarian who had recently retired. While at first he was very happy at not having to show up at work every morning, he gradually began to get bored and then depressed. The days passed slowly; he felt useless and no longer had a reason for

Some "mourners" turn their anger on themselves.

living. When he talked to me about it, I asked him if he had grieved the loss of his library. My question intrigued him, and took him by surprise. Then I invited him to go and bid farewell to the central catalogue that he had helped to create during his 30 years of service. He followed my advice. Hidden from view between two tall bookstacks, he said goodbye to the place to which he had consecrated his time, his work, his devotion. He was surprised at the tears he shed. His tears were not for things he had left behind, but rather for what they represented: 30 years of dedication and a job that had made him happy.

The grieving person also experiences feelings of subdued *anger*, likely to take various forms: irritability, discontent, impatience, frustration and so forth. This is a disguised protest against the cruel absence of a loved one, an ideal, an activity or simply an object. It is not unusual, for example, to hear immigrants sharply criticize their adopted country. A lady from Italy confided to me once that the flowers in Canada simply had no fragrance compared to flowers in Italy. A man I met said that Canadians are not very hospitable. These people had clearly not grieved the loss of their country of origin.

Some "mourners" turn their anger on themselves. They experience a feeling of guilt, which they often then cultivate. Some feel they haven't done enough with their lives. Others blame themselves for not having loved enough their dear one whom they have now lost. Retired people may feel guilty about leaving friends at the workplace and have the impression that they have abandoned them. Newly divorced people tend to look back nostalgically on past happiness and hate themselves for not having been more tolerant towards their ex-spouse.

The emotional release draws to a close when the "great lament" takes place. The grieving person suddenly becomes conscious of the definitive loss of the loved person or thing. They let go of their last hope of reconnecting with them or of going backward in time. The "great lament" can be identified by the intensity of the pain that is expressed in weeping and even moaning. After this intense emotional release, the bereaved person usually experiences a deep peace, sometimes even mystical states.

Once the emotional work of letting go is well underway, the grieving person must move to action.

4. Assuming the tasks related to bereavement

Once the emotional work of letting go is well underway, the grieving person must move to action and handle the business related to the separation. In the case of a relative's death, for example, there are inheritance matters to be settled, burial arrangements to be made (according to the appropriate cultural rites) and promises made to the deceased to be kept. Retirees must do their leave-taking, empty their workplace of their personal belongings, reorganize their time and their activities, complete the usual forms, sometimes even make new friends to replace their colleagues at work, and so on. The tasks to be completed vary with the type of separation. These activities, which may appear insignificant, will help accelerate the whole process of letting go.

5. Discovering the meaning of the loss

Expressing feelings and completing the tasks related to bereavement allow the person to develop a certain amount of detachment from the break that has occurred and to see it in its true perspective. To resolve their grief, they will have to discover what choices will allow them to pursue their

Frequently a wound becomes the opportunity for people to discover their mission.

path in life. Rather than remaining impoverished and crushed, they are now in a position to benefit from the increased maturity that their loss has allowed them to acquire. Here are some examples of positive stances people took following their loss. For some of them, it was their mission that had just been clearly revealed to them.

A woman abandoned by her husband found herself penniless; this misfortune pushed her to complete her nursing program, a dream she had cherished since childhood and which she had not been able to fulfill while raising her family. A dance teacher who learned she had multiple sclerosis realized her dancing career was over. But she asserted that this did not mean her life was over. She set about realizing her second dream, which was to create software for exercises to help people learn English. A young man became a paraplegic after a motorcycle accident; during his rehabilitation, he discovered that he was good at electronics. A man suffering from a great disappointment in love was amazed to find himself writing poetry, for he had never thought of himself as having any literary talent. His distress had forced him to get in touch with his emotions and to develop his poetic gift. Frequently a wound becomes the opportunity for people to discover their mission. This will be discussed in greater detail in the next chapter.

6. Asking and granting forgiveness

Forgiveness is an excellent means of letting go. My personal experience has allowed me to note its importance in the grieving process. To properly grieve for a person we have lost, either through death or otherwise, it is important to forgive that person. Anyone who thinks it is possible to leave a relationship, a situation or a place of work with resentment, bitterness or subdued anger in their heart is holding on to an illusion, for the baggage they cart around with them will be very heavy.

One day, a man asked a former prisoner of war whether he had forgiven his torturers. He declared that he would never forgive them. The man then responded, "So they still have you in prison, then!"

To properly grieve for a person we have lost, it is important to forgive that person.

7. Claiming your legacy

The final stage of resolving your grief consists of recovering the affection you lavished on the person you loved or on a precious activity or object. In other words, the legacy results from reclaiming the affection, hopes, dreams and expectations invested in the beloved. Here is an example. A friend of mine had just left her position as manager of a social services agency. I invited her to claim the legacy of the investment she had made during her 15 years of work there. She came up with the following ritual for the farewell celebration organized for her. At the end of the evening, she opened up the suitcase she had been given as a parting gift, and then told her colleagues that she did not want to leave without taking along with her all the beautiful moments they had lived together. Then she pretended to take her secretary's hands and place them in her suitcase, thus indicating her desire to lay claim to her spirit of service. She did the same thing with her assistant's smile, which she saw as the symbol of her good humour; with the shoulders of another, signifying the courage he had displayed in his work; and so on for each of her colleagues. At the end, she closed the suitcase and said that she was leaving with her suitcase filled with all the wealth of her time spent among them.

If people who are grieving can find listeners who can be present and attentive, they will be able to share their experience, be released from their emotional burden and recover their psychological equilibrium.

How do you finally let go?

The most effective way to finally let go is to tell the story of your loss and to express the emotions you experienced as you went through it. If people who are grieving can find listeners who can be present and attentive, they will be able to share their experience, be released from their emotional burden and recover their psychological equilibrium.

To be able to let go, it is important to evaluate honestly the seriousness of our loss. This can be done by answering the following questions: "What did this person represent for me?" or "What energy did I invest in this person or this reality?" Thus, we can measure the subjective value of what has been lost. This awareness, painful as it may be, enables us to enter more deeply into our grief and resolve it as quickly as possible.

Rituals for letting go

A ritual is a theatre of the soul in which we carry out in a symbolic way the change we want to see produced in our life. It has the power to indicate to the unconscious what it must do to be liberated from the past. Living a ritual with friends sometimes helps us to achieve the detachment that will subsequently allow us to take on our mission. Here are a few examples.

Seeking inner detachment from events of the past, one of my friends started to clean out his attic, his basement and his garage. Another man, to symbolize clearly that he would have to give up a very lucrative job to realize his mission, deliberately burned a $10 bill. Someone else wanted to be freed from a false belief inculcated by her father. She had been made to believe that she was responsible for the death of her mother, who had died giving birth to her. To be liberated from this family secret, she gathered a few friends for a ritual. First she had them bind her arms and legs, to show them how her father had for a long time paralyzed her with this false belief. Then, with a pair of scissors that she could barely manage to handle, she succeeded in cutting the ropes that bound her, to signify to her father that he would no longer exert any influence over her.

A woman had to have a hysterectomy, which ended all hope of biological motherhood for her. So she decided to act out a ritual to help her enter this new stage of her life. First, she asked the surgeon to conserve her uterus in formalin. Once she had recovered from the surgery, she gathered for a rite of passage with some friends at a farm belonging to one of them. She wanted to symbolize that since physical maternity had now become impossible, she would become a spiritual mother for her clients in psychotherapy. She dug a deep hole in which she buried her uterus. Then, on top of it, she planted a tree to symbolize her new motherhood.

A woman decided to act out a ritual to help her enter this new stage of her life.

Sometimes we turn towards God,
when our foundations are trembling,
only to learn
that it is this self-same God
who is shaking them.

– ANONYMOUS

CHAPTER 5

Healing Your Wounds to Discover Your Mission

In workshops on the theme Discovering Your Mission, several participants felt, to my great surprise, that they could not identify their life project, as they were too preoccupied with past wounds. They could not get through the letting-go stage to concentrate on discovering their identity. I really had to stress the amount of time that must be devoted to letting go. In fact, it is important not just to say goodbye, but also to heal your wounds through forgiveness.

It is important not just to say goodbye, but also to heal your wounds through forgiveness.

The following examples of people "wounded by life" illustrate clearly the kinds of blocks that can impede the pursuit of our mission:

- A young woman who was a victim of date rape does not forgive herself for having exposed herself to a dangerous situation. She no longer trusts men because, for her, they are all potential rapists.
- A young man abandoned by his father no longer feels capable of pursuing his calling to a helping profession.
- A woman still in the throes of disappointed love believes she will never again be able to love, never again be able to participate in building a couple's life.
- A businessman takes a self-deprecating attitude when his company goes bankrupt; he remains bitter towards his creditors for he sees them all as sharks who would not give him the slightest chance to straighten out his situation.

It is not unusual for people who are suffering to feel powerless to heal themselves and rebuild their future. They are inclined to vegetate in resentment, constantly reliving the pain of the injury they sustained. They stay stuck in a painful past that ruins their present and prevents them from

Psychologists are discovering more and more clearly the healing value of forgiveness.

envisioning a promising future. The fear of being hurt again haunts them and closes them off from all prospects of risk and success. They have lost faith in themselves and no longer see how they can realize their dream. The search for their mission will prove impossible as long as their wound is not healed.

We shall highlight, first of all, the need to embark on a process of forgiving ourselves and others in order to heal and be liberated from injuries we have suffered. Secondly, we will emphasize that owning our wound and properly tending to it allows us to discover a new meaning to our life and our mission.

HEALING YOUR WOUNDS THROUGH FORGIVENESS

Psychologists are discovering more and more clearly the healing value of forgiveness. Surveys done on people who practise forgiveness in order to heal have shown that they are far less prone to anxiety, depression and fits of anger. They also have significantly greater self-esteem. These scientifically verified therapeutic effects are lasting and prolonged over several years (Enright, 1998: 58-59, 71). It will be useful to recall here briefly the stages of forgiveness presented in my book *How to Forgive: A Step-by-Step Guide.*

Step 1. Decide to not seek revenge and to put a stop to the offensive actions

The choice to forgive begins with a firm decision to not seek revenge and to end the hurt.

It is important to develop an attitude of forgiveness rather than to decide each time we are hurt whether we will forgive. Even beforehand, we must guard against the instinct to seek revenge. In fact, the idea of revenge is so spontaneous that it will win out over any wavering desire to forgive.

The choice to forgive begins with an act of courage.

When we think about committing revenge, we usually think of all sorts of violent acts; that is the active form of revenge. There is also a passive form of revenge, which feeds on a silent anger that prevents us from living and letting those around us live. We see it in depression, nostalgia, despondency, lack of initiative and enthusiasm, apathy, lack of feeling, a constant state of indefinable boredom, etc. What a useless expenditure of energy! Thus we poison our own life and the lives of our family and friends.

Now, the decision not to "make the offender pay" does not mean that we allow these misdeeds to continue. On the contrary, we must use all our assertive power to end violence in a non-violent manner. (Resorting to violence would be to yield to the instinct for revenge.)

Some have accused those who forgive of being faint-hearted. They would be right if the victims failed to protest against the offender. The choice to forgive is in no way a cowardly act; quite the opposite is true. It begins with an act of courage and protest against any form of being victimized. Otherwise, forgiveness would be nothing more than a con game.

Step 2. Recognize your pain and poverty

Injured persons who stubbornly forget the offence, excuse the offender and deny wounded emotions will never be able to forgive. Without becoming masochists or complacent victims, they must acknowledge both the offence and the wound. If they do not do this, the offence they suffered will continue to do terrible damage to their sensitivity and their

To become more aware of the full impact of the offence on you, there is no more effective method than to confide in someone.

emotions. It will drain their energy without them even realizing it. To deny or pretend to deny their wound blocks any possibility of forgiveness. In fact, this strategy of denial only ends up burying the wound in the unconscious. All that remains on the conscious level is a vague uneasiness, a type of depression, sudden irritability or a crazy wish to forget everything.

Step 3. Share your pain with someone

To become more aware of the full impact of the offence on you, there is no more effective method than to confide in someone. If the offender appears ready to take responsibility, then that is the person you need to speak to first. There is a good chance that you will be quite ready to forgive the offender. An old proverb in fact says, "An error admitted is already half forgiven."

Unfortunately, the offender is not always ready to admit responsibility: sometimes it is impossible to reach him or her. In these cases, the best thing to do is to meet with a sympathetic person who is capable of listening to the story of your ordeal. Numerous benefits will result: you will see your painful situation in a different light; you will experience great relief at sharing the weight of your sorrow; you will feel more empowered to find creative solutions; and you will discover within yourself more courage to implement them.

Step 4. Clearly identify what has been lost so you can grieve it

Under the shock of an offence, it sometimes happens that we cannot tell just what part of us has been hurt. We often have the impression that our whole person has been grazed. The illusion that we have been seriously injured makes us powerless to react and prevents us from taking the smallest step towards forgiveness. We must at all costs avoid revelling in our victim state. We must instead apply ourselves to determining the true nature of the wound. A few questions will help with this process: "Just what part of me was wounded? Was the injury to my dignity, to one of my qualities, to my self-esteem, to my pride, to my love for my family, to my material possessions?" Often an old childhood wound that has not yet healed will surface. Your ability to determine the nature and extent of the wound without exaggerating will allow you to grieve more easily.

Often an old childhood wound that has not yet healed will surface.

Step 5. Accept your anger and desire for revenge

One of the major difficulties encountered on the path to forgiveness is knowing how to manage our anger. It takes on many forms: the camouflaged forms of frustration, discontent, disappointment or irritation, or the form of explosive anger, wrath, fury or even rage. When our anger is not channelled, we risk creating serious blocks within ourselves and we become "passive aggressive." We find ourselves bothered by constant inner dialogue, haunted by resentment and obsessed by fantasies of revenge. If we turn our anger against ourselves, we risk being tormented by a strong feeling of guilt. If this feeling is projected onto others, we will be unfairly wounding innocent people – often those closest to us. Finally, we will project our aggression on to those around us; we will be afraid not just of the aggression of others but of our own aggressivity as well.

Ideally, managing our anger well consists of acknowledging its presence, owning it and expressing it constructively. Instead of repressing it, we need to use it to protest the bad treatment we received from the offender.

When we forgive ourselves, we stop being our own torturer.

Anger is not, in itself, a negative emotion, as we have often been led to believe. On the contrary, it protects our integrity when it is threatened. Once it is expressed fairly, it will diminish and then give way to another underlying emotion, usually sadness. The emergence of sadness makes it possible to engage in grief work and, eventually, to forgive.

Step 6. Forgive yourself

Any serious offence sets in motion a curious mechanism: the victim instinctively identifies with the perpetrator, imitates the offending behaviour and continues to injure him- or herself. For this reason, this stage represents a turning point in the process of forgiveness. When we forgive ourselves, we stop being our own torturer.

To recreate our inner harmony, we have to stop accusing ourselves and reproaching ourselves: "I should have known! How could I have allowed myself to love such a person? Why am I always drawn towards these kinds of situations? I must be a masochist, a fool, naturally stupid!" All this blame directed at ourselves halts any progress towards forgiveness. That's why it is so important to change our inner dialogue and to learn to be kind and gentle with ourselves, as we would be with our best friend in a comparable situation.

Forgiving ourselves will restore the harmony between the two parties in us: the one that took the place of the offender and the one that is the victim. On one hand, we must transform our internalized tormenter into a protector to defuse the violence we are experiencing and, on the other hand, we must re-establish the victim's dignity. (To learn how to create this harmony, see my book *How to Forgive*, especially the exercise for restoring inner harmony on pp. 125-133.)

Step 7. Start to understand the offender

It would not be wise to undertake this step without first having restored our inner wholeness. In fact, only when the harmony within us has returned will we be able to approach the offender to face this person calmly and serenely. Otherwise, we are laying ourselves open to becoming lost in confusion.

Making the effort to understand the offender in no way means that we are trying to excuse the offensive behaviour or, worse, condone it.

Making the effort to understand the offender in no way means that we are trying to excuse the offensive behaviour or, worse, condone it. We are seeking instead to put it back into context, so we can explain it better. To do this, we may ask ourselves the following questions: "In what circumstances did the person commit the offence? What could explain such an action on their part? Their own history of woundedness? Their own setbacks, failures and disappointments?" Acquiring all this information about the offender will help mitigate the severity with which we judge them.

Understanding the offender better also allows us to separate the person from the deed and keeps us from demonizing them forever. By not identifying the offender with the wrong action and by believing that he or she is capable of change, we can perhaps see the offender in a different light: as a weak person, capable of evolving and eventually repenting.

Step 8. Discover what the pain means in your life

The preceding stages are necessary to ensure our emotional healing. Having made it to this point, we now have to detach from and stand back from our emotional experience without denying it. This distancing will allow us to better situate the offence within the whole of our lives and to draw from it a meaning that assures us of a reason for living.

The 12th and final step addresses what follows forgiveness: we ask ourselves whether it is better to end this relationship or renew it.

Given the importance of this stage for spiritual healing, I have dedicated a special section to it at the very end of this chapter: "Missions that are born of our losses and wounds."

Steps 9 to 12

Steps 9 to 11 are of a more spiritual nature: we know that we deserve forgiveness and that we are already forgiven; we stop trying to forgive; we open ourselves up to the grace of forgiveness. The 12th and final step addresses what follows forgiveness: we ask ourselves whether it is better to end this relationship or renew it.

Here, then, is the list of what we must do to achieve true forgiveness:

1. Decide to not seek revenge and to put a stop to the offensive actions.
2. Recognize our pain and inner poverty.
3. Share our pain with someone.
4. Clearly identify what has been lost so we can grieve it.
5. Accept our anger and desire for revenge.
6. Forgive ourselves.
7. Start to understand the offender.
8. Discover what the pain means in our life.
9. Know that we are worthy of forgiveness and are already forgiven.
10. Stop trying so hard to forgive.
11. Open up to the grace of forgiveness.
12. Decide whether to end the relationship or to renew it.

Looking to your spiritual resources

The process of healing a wound, as described in the preceding stages, prepares the heart to forgive. But that is only the start of forgiveness. Forgiveness, or pardon, signifies the perfect gift, for the Latin root of the word "pardon" *(per* and *donare)* means "to give completely." Now, a gift like this, requiring perfect love, largely exceeds human capacity! We could say, "To avenge is human; to forgive, divine." Forgiveness lies beyond all efforts of human will, no matter how generous or magnanimous a person's heart may be. It demands an overabundance of love, a special grace that can only come from God. The traditional religions are unanimous in recognizing this: "Only God can forgive."

In the world of psychology, we wonder today whether forgiveness is possible without God's help. Some humanist psychologists say yes; they see forgiveness as simply a therapeutic technique. I cannot accept this because it reduces forgiveness to a method of healing, which would distract from its true goal: to allow us to love our enemies. What makes us capable of the high degree of generosity required for forgiveness is the deep sense of being unconditionally loved and forgiven by God. How can we love if we do not feel that we have been loved? Likewise, how can we forgive if we do not have the deep conviction that we ourselves have been forgiven?

People who forgive enjoy a divine grace that confers on them a very special love exceeding all human love. It allows them to forgive. In fact, their forgiveness only echoes the forgiveness first granted to them by God. To a certain extent, forgiving persons are not the authors of their forgiveness, but the subject of divine forgiveness. Only the power of forgiveness received from God makes the human person capable of forgiving in turn.

In short, forgiveness is the fruit of collaboration between human effort and divine gift. It keeps us from

What makes us capable of the high degree of generosity required for forgiveness is the deep sense of being unconditionally loved and forgiven by God.

Viktor Frankl concluded that the desire to give meaning to life — rather than the desire for pleasure or the will to power — controls the human spirit.

becoming trapped by the desire for revenge; it makes us become aware of our wound and heals it; it restores our self-esteem and confidence in our resources; it reminds us that God's grace empowers us to make things new. Forgiveness opens up the future and makes it possible to realize our mission.

MISSIONS THAT ARE BORN FROM OUR LOSSES AND WOUNDS

Viktor Frankl did not share Freud's "pansexualism," the view that the pleasure principle was the main motivation in human behaviour. During the Second World War, Frankl spent time in the Nazi concentration camps. He emerged convinced that the only reason he had not committed suicide was that life had a meaning and it was up to him to discover it. He concluded that the desire to give meaning to life — rather than the desire for pleasure or the will to power — controls the human spirit. Regarding the prisoners in the concentration camps, he wrote, "Woe to [the one] who saw no more sense in [their] life, no aim, no purpose, and therefore no point in carrying on. [They were] soon lost" (1965:121). He added that, however great the suffering one is subjected to, it is always possible to find a reason for being or for living.

The void created by the absence of a loved one or by the loss of something precious eventually demands to be filled. To live fully, and not just exist, the "mourner" or "victim" can and must find a new meaning to their life. After the death of her husband, a client confided to me, "My life is like a book with blank pages. I don't know how to fill them anymore." Then I asked her what title she would give her book. After a moment's hesitation, she exclaimed, "Onward and Upward, Michelle!"

It is quite amazing and even paradoxical that loss or injury often provides the springboard for discovering a new orientation in life. Our calling emerges from our losses, setbacks and disappointments. I am thinking of a woman who had been the victim of domestic violence and founded a home for battered women; a couple whose son was killed by a reckless drunk driver who made it their mission to force the authorities to pay more attention to punishing drunk drivers; a paraplegic who spent most of his time raising funds to help other disabled people. There are endless examples of people whose mission springs from situations like these.

Loss or injury often provides the springboard for discovering a new orientation in life.

People with a special disability or those who have a chronic illness often prove to be the best at assisting others. They have founded the majority of the organizations for mutual co-operation in society. Following a misfortune, they looked within for personal resources, of which they had often been unaware, and discovered the wherewithal to heal themselves and help others heal. These people are better able to understand those who suffer from a similar condition. They know the path to healing. You might say they have been initiated into the calling of "wounded healer."

Although many people have found a new reason for living after a major ordeal, many others become depressed, play the martyr, hold on to their spite and contemplate suicide. When people choose to live in these emotional states, they end up being the losers. In a lecture I gave in Paris, I had just finished stating that it was possible to find a new meaning to one's life after the death of a loved one. I was then subjected to the wrath of a mother whose child had died. She attacked all caregivers, doctors and

Discovering our mission following an ordeal allows us to experience a new inner freedom and to sight new horizons.

psychologists as well. She seemed to be more interested in glorying in the public display of her anger as a tearful mother than in grieving for her child and finding meaning in her suffering. I thought to myself that such rage sustained against caregivers and family members would sooner or later perversely affect the health of another family member. My prediction proved accurate when I learned that another of her children subsequently died of leukemia.

I am certainly not advocating the denial of the misfortunes that befall us. But, as Viktor Frankl reminds us in *Man's Search for Meaning*, it is always possible to modify our attitude in the face of misfortune so that we might live it better. In *The Soul's Code*, James Hillman writes that we must not so much ask ourselves why this thing happened to us or what we did to bring it upon ourselves, but rather what our angel expects of us now.

Discovering our mission following an ordeal allows us to experience a new inner freedom and to sight new horizons. We emerge enriched by an experience that could have destroyed us. We are more sensitive to the calls of our mission. We see more clearly how our actions can bring to others who are afflicted the hope they need.

To help you find a new reason for living following a great hardship, I suggest you answer the series of questions below. The purpose of these questions is to transform the hurt into tenderness, openness to others and the discovery of a personal mission.

• *What have I learned from my grief or the offence I suffered?*

• *What new resources for life have I discovered within myself?*

• *What limitations or vulnerable areas have I discovered in myself? How was I able to handle them?*

• *Have I become more human and compassionate towards others?*

• *What new level of maturity have I reached?*

• *What have I been initiated into by this trial?*

• *What new reasons for living have I given myself?*

• *To what extent have I decided to change my relationship with others and, more particularly, with God?*

• *How will I now pursue the course of my life?*

What new reasons for living have I given myself?

PART THREE

The Neutral Zone

O cursèd winter... O cursèd wandering! So much time
lost not knowing what to do anymore: emptiness,
in-betweenness, blur, discomfort, indecision,
stagnation, doubt, hesitation, fog,
uncertainty ... Empty time, lost time ...
O cursèd wandering! Be over now ...
Be gone ... at last!

Why such homage paid to winter,
to that cessation time, to that essential wandering!
Cursèd season or unloved season?
Despicable season or despised season?
Misunderstood season? Season to discover?
Season to befriend.

MICHELLE ROBERGE

CHAPTER 6

The Dark, Liminal Period

Having completed your grieving and forgiving, you enter into a liminal period. It is an essential stage of deepening your identity and, subsequently, of discovering your mission. The temptation to avoid this uncomfortable time is strong because, by all appearances, it is useless and empty.

A number of spiritual traditions recommend this in-between period of solitude, silence and meditation.

Inspired by the work of anthropologist Van Gennep in *The Rites of Passage*, William Bridges proposes a three-part model of transition: letting go, which consists of disengaging oneself from the previous state; the neutral or liminal period; and reincorporation into the community. Van Gennep had observed this transition pattern in the initiation rites of traditional societies. After future initiates were separated from their families, their initiators required that they spend a period of time, called "liminal time," in seclusion. During this time they were made to die symbolically to childhood and taught their roles as women or men.

A number of spiritual traditions recommend this in-between period of solitude, silence and meditation. Neophytes withdraw from all their daily activities, from the constant influx of information, from their worries, social commitments, roles and the expectations of those around them. This retreat into solitude and silence allows them to become aware of their identity and, gradually, of their mission. This is why great figures who were called to carry out an important mission gave themselves a liminal period so they could answer the question "Who am I?" and reflect on their call. Think of Jesus, who spent 40 days in the desert to become aware of his identity as Son of God before undertaking his mission.

Psychologically, this transition stage is one of hesitation, apparent inactivity, even confusion, emptiness, "spiritual incubation" and exploration.

The nature of the liminal period

The strength of William Bridges' work is that he highlights this in-between period, which is often forgotten today by people "in transition" who are too preoccupied with getting over their grief and throwing themselves into a new adventure. He refers to it as "the neutral zone," because nothing seems to happen there. Other authors have several different names for it: the in-between period, the liminal period, the essential wandering; more poetically, it is likened to winter. Indeed, it seems to be a cold, frozen time, sterile and non-productive in appearance.

Psychologically, this transition stage is one of hesitation, apparent inactivity, even confusion, emptiness, "spiritual incubation" and exploration. We live a quiet uneasiness; we cling desperately to the past or try to escape into the future. We feel we're just spinning our wheels, going nowhere; it even seems we're not real anymore. Here are a few examples: we've just been let go from our job, we've just left a position that included a certain social prestige, we've just separated from our spouse, our children have just left home or we have just learned we're in poor health. From now on, our identity cannot be determined by our social relationships; we have lost those specific points of reference to knowing just who we are. Despite all appearances, here is a moment of grace being offered us so that we can see ourselves in a truer light and explore our deeper identity.

In her book *Tant d'hiver au coeur du changement* [So much winter at the heart of change], Michelle Roberge describes the liminal period: "The more I work, experience, live, discover and deepen this idea of 'wandering,' this season of transition, the more I become aware of its mysterious, amazing, disconcerting and yet always fascinating character" (1998:119) [Translation]. As it is uncomfortable, this period usually frightens us. We would rather deny it or skip it. It has the distinctive feature of making us feel we are in a void, like the one experienced by the trapeze artist who has let go of one trapeze and is in mid-air waiting for the other one, which does not show up instantly. We are disoriented for a stretch of time, not knowing what to hang on to in order to resolve our identity crisis.

This period enables us to explore our interiority and allow the great dream of our life to rise up within us.

An obligatory passage towards rediscovery and reorientation

This period of wavering, far from being futile, is an obligatory passage towards rediscovery and reorientation. William Bridges has given it an important function, based on his knowledge of the stages of change. This period enables us to explore our interiority and allow the great dream of our life to rise up within us. Winter, though seemingly sterile, is a fruitful period when gestation is taking place. It is a time of mysterious creativity. As with any work of creation, discovering our mission depends on a certain period of ripening, of incubation. The artist who drives away the muse of inspiration will produce only a superficial and commonplace work; this is how it is with creating our mission. We must live for some considerable time in confusion before we can have an original, clear idea of our mission.

Advice for living the liminal period well

The spiritual masters know this psychological desert well: it leaves the subjects feeling as if they are dying. They recommend several methods to help us to handle this

The neutral zone is an ideal time to allow the shadow of the personality to emerge.

liminal time better. If we have the patience to stay with it, the desert will begin to flower.

- Make a retreat. Give yourself some time out to separate from your daily concerns.
- Seek out peaceful surroundings: for example, a place in nature where you can observe a stream, plants and animals, which invites you to be patient.
- Choose solitude and, in the silence, learn to tune out the chatter of your interior dialogue and tune in to the aspirations of your soul.
- Do "inner work" exercises; keep a journal; write your life story; pray for help; and so on.
- Pray to have a new vision of your mission; allow the dream of an ideal to rise within you.
- Make a pilgrimage. The pilgrimage symbolizes the soul on a journey towards attainment of a spiritual goal.

Some friends of mine who walked for over a month on a pilgrimage to Santiago de Compostela in Spain said they felt their souls being laid bare completely, an experience that allowed them to come into direct contact with their shadow, their hidden side. The neutral zone is an ideal time to allow the shadow of the personality to emerge. Here are some concrete, practical exercises that can help you explore and reintegrate your shadow.

THE SHADOW: THAT TREASURE BURIED BY FEAR

What is the shadow?

The shadow is everything that we have driven back into the unconscious for fear of being rejected by the important people in our lives. We suppressed certain behaviours or aspects of our personality so as not to lose their affection, disappoint them or make them uncomfortable. We soon learned to discern what was acceptable in their eyes and what was not. So, in order not to displease them, we eagerly relegated large portions of ourselves to the faraway realms of the unconscious. We did our utmost to evade the slightest verbal or tacit disapproval on their part.

The shadow is the antithesis of the ideal self, called the "persona": that faculty of adaptation that always pushes us to meet the expectations of our environment and, more particularly, the expectations of our educators. The persona thinks it must repress important aspects of its personality in the unconscious or, as poet Robert Bly puts it, "stuff them into one's garbage bag." Bly says that until we are 30, we fill our bag to please others and to be accepted by them. And later, we have to empty it out to recover everything that we had thrown in.

The shadow and mission

The shadow holds the key to our mission. It is closer to our true self, our spiritual centre, than the persona is. The persona, by contrast, pays more attention to the expectations of those around us. Closer to the Self, the shadow reflects more closely the aspirations of the deepest self. To gain better self-knowledge, it is important to pull out of the "garbage bag" the undeveloped, unknown or rejected parts of ourselves. On that condition can we discover the deep desires of our being and, consequently, what we are called to as individuals.

The shadow holds the key to our mission.

Unfocused energy constitutes a major obstacle to discerning our mission.

The reintegration of your shadow: an asset in the search for your mission

The exercise of reintegrating the shadow is not so much aimed at discovering who *I am* as learning who *we are* with our "sub-personalities." We are, in fact, plural beings. You no doubt feel you have a single personality. But it sometimes surprises us that with certain people, we are no longer quite ourselves. It is almost as if we were taking on another personality. In reality, our many-sided personality reveals various aspects of ourselves according to the situation and the circumstances.

The obstacle that we most frequently encounter in discovering our mission comes from the fragmentation of our identity into "sub-personalities." Because each wants to go its own particular way, we disperse our energy instead of concentrating it. This happens with many young adults who cannot make up their minds as they are pulled in different directions by various voices: their father's expectations, their mother's aspirations, their friends' wishes, invitations from all sides, the appeal of consumerism, and so forth. As a result of having spent too much time listening to others, they have stopped listening to the voice of their own deep desire. Some very talented young people don't know how to choose from the overwhelming number of options available to them. I knew a young man who simply could not settle on a choice among his countless aspirations: he wanted to be a priest, he loved electronics, he had artistic talent . . . . Finally, he just did nothing, for he felt that to make a choice would limit him.

Unfocused energy, then, constitutes a major obstacle to discerning our mission. In contrast, the work of getting our various "sub-personalities" to converge creates in us a synergy that sheds new light on our mission and gives us the courage to follow it.

To better understand the shadow and its riches, here is a series of exercises that will help you, first of all, to grasp and identify the various facets of your shadow and, second, to reintegrate them. Those who are interested in learning more about this subject may wish to consult my book *How to Befriend Your Shadow: Welcoming Your Unloved Side.*

Getting to know your shadow, which has crystallized in your subconscious over several years, is no small matter.

GETTING TO KNOW YOUR SHADOW

Getting to know your shadow, which has crystallized in your subconscious over several years, is no small matter. It often happens that, as we approach it, we feel confused and somewhat disoriented. We must proceed in this work cautiously and humbly, undertaking it only when we feel emotionally stable and, preferably, when someone we trust can accompany us.

The following is a series of questions that will enable you to sketch a profile of the various aspects of your shadow. Enter your answers in your notebook. You can then summarize in your *Journal of My Discoveries* what you have discovered about your mission.

Question 1

• What are the most flattering aspects of your social ego that you would like to see recognized by others?

Once you have singled out a particular aspect of your persona, ask yourself what quality or character trait you had to repress in order to be appreciated or loved. For example, if you wanted to be recognized as a gentle, generous and friendly person, you probably had to hide

The topics on which you are evasive will reveal your fear of unmasking a side of yourself that you consider embarrassing.

your aggressiveness, your selfishness and your fits of bad temper. These qualities or character traits that you were led to downplay make up various facets of your shadow.

Dare now to recognize their value and legitimacy. Do so by telling yourself, "I have the right to my fighting spirit; I have the right to seek my own well-being; I have a right to my bad temper." While you are making these statements, be attentive to the emotions you experience. They will vary considerably from one person to the next. Some will say to themselves, "I feel confused"; others, "I feel guilty and ashamed"; still others will say, "I feel completely energized."

With this exercise you will have begun to befriend your shadow.

Question 2

• What topic(s) of discussion do you tend to avoid in your conversations with people? Sexuality, aggressiveness, faith, ambitions, incompetence …?

Whatever they are, you can be sure that the topics on which you are evasive will reveal your fear of unmasking a side of yourself that you consider embarrassing. Unless you have complete confidence in your conversation partner, you will feel very ill-at-ease broaching these subjects. The day you do manage to broach them with a discreet and trustworthy person, you will have begun to "nibble at" your shadow.

Question 3

• In what situations do you find yourself becoming nervous, over-sensitive or defensive? By what types of remarks are you taken aback?

Are you surprised at how strongly you react? If so, this is an indication that someone has just stepped on a piece of your shadow, on a personality zone that you do not wish to reveal. Your level of discomfort and your extreme reaction obviously show that a part of yourself you wanted to keep hidden has just been unmasked.

A violent reaction signals that a facet of your shadow has just been exposed.

Question 4

• In what circumstances do you feel inferior or lacking in self-confidence? Do you sometimes feel inadequate – that is, not sufficiently competent, articulate, intelligent, discreet?

This is the sign of a shadow wanting to come to the surface. During my student years, I once lived with a group made up mainly of artists. I had a hard time understanding why I was constantly uncomfortable in that community, until finally it occurred to me that I had neglected and even repressed any artistic expression of my own.

Question 5

• Are you inclined to be offended when you are criticized? What kinds of criticism do you find annoying or even irritating?

A violent reaction signals that a facet of your shadow has just been exposed. If people close to you repeatedly criticize you for the same thing, and if each time you react in the same sharp manner, it means that they are exposing a masked side of your personality that you really do not want to show.

Such an extreme reaction could also have another explanation: you may have the impression that you are being

Accepting your imperfections, weaknesses, shortcomings and mistakes shows that you have begun to befriend your shadow.

made the scapegoat for a group of people. In that case, you would need to ask yourself what it is in you that could have made others choose you as the depository of the collective shadow of the group.

Question 6

• With what aspects of yourself do you feel upset or dissatisfied? For example, are you unhappy with your physical appearance or one of your character traits?

If so, you are probably trying to conceal some actual shortcoming or something that you consider to be a weakness. It is very likely in this case that your persona is imposing on you an ideal of success, beauty or perfection that you believe is impossible to attain.

Accepting your imperfections, weaknesses, shortcomings and mistakes shows that you have begun to befriend your shadow. This indicates that you are acquiring the beginnings of wisdom, otherwise known as humility.

Question 7

• What trait distinguished your family from other families in your neighbourhood or area?

Every family has its own characteristic. For example, people would say about the Monbourquettes, "They're honest folk"; about the Robinsons, "They show a lot of courage"; about the Smiths, "They are really hard workers"; about the Lucianos, "They're so hospitable." To know your family shadow, find the opposite trait to the one that people attributed to your family. For example, for a family to maintain its reputation of honesty, they would have been obliged to give up the use of shrewdness or diplomacy; to maintain their reputation of being courageous, they would have had to repress any manifestation of fear; to keep their reputation as hard-working, they would have had to forgo a lot of fun and recreation; to keep being seen as hospitable, they would have had to deny themselves the family intimacy they would have liked to preserve.

You will recognize your family shadow in the behaviours your family did not allow itself to engage in or express.

You will recognize your family shadow in the behaviours your family did not allow itself to engage in or express.

Question 8

• Is there someone who gets on your nerves, really irritates you, drives you up the wall?

You can be sure that you are projecting part of your shadow onto them. Take time to identify clearly in that person the aspect of his or her personality that provokes such antipathy in you. To do this, look closely at how this trait annoys or irritates you. For example, you abhor someone's vulgarity because this clashes with your taste for distinction and discretion. Then ask yourself whether, to bring moderation to your over-sensitivity and your excessive politeness, you might not benefit from learning to be more direct and more straightforward in affirming yourself. You don't need to lapse into vulgarity, but you could be more frank in the way you approach people. You can retain your courteous and distinguished manner and offset any tendency to be extreme in these qualities by having greater self-confidence and even by being bolder. You will then become a person who is more whole than perfect.

*An unknown shadow
becomes mean and
aggressive; one that
is acknowledged and
accepted will become
a precious ally.*

REINTEGRATING THE SHADOW

You no doubt have recognized in yourself several facets of
your shadow. I will now propose ways for you to reintegrate
them. Take your time and reintegrate just one aspect of your
shadow at a time.

The first condition necessary for the reintegration of a
facet of your shadow is the ability to name it. You will be
surprised at how, once you have given it a name, you will
have a firmer hold on it. Identifying it is already a way of
accepting it. An unknown shadow becomes mean and
aggressive; one that is acknowledged and accepted will
become a precious ally.

What up until now seemed "demonic" and threatening
in your shadow will thus be transformed into a *daimon*, that
is, a "good genius" who fosters your growth and full self-
realization. It was a precious asset for me to meet up with
my "ignorant" side, the one who does not yet know
everything but is keen to do so. Thus, I was able to reconcile
my "omniscient" side with my "ignorant" side. Because
they have stopped warring with each other, both can now
contribute to my growth as a person.

Another way to reintegrate your shadow is to imagine a
dialogue with a person whom you dislike or who irritates
you. Start by addressing the person and expressing what you
do not like or what you fear in him or her. Then, put yourself
in the other person's place and reply. Gradually you will gain
the impression that you are forming a co-operative
relationship. Continue the dialogue; you may even try to
negotiate an exchange of qualities or character traits with
him or her. For example, if the other person is very
combative, ask them for some of their fighting spirit; from
your side, offer to lend some of your gentleness and docility.

Once you have completed these exchanges, thank the other person for having taught you traits that will likely enrich your own personality. This approach both teaches you to respect your "enemy" and provides you with an opportunity to grow personally.

In a third strategy for reintegrating your shadow, you create two opposite symbols that you will unite in a third symbol. This exercise was inspired by Berta's theory.

In a third strategy for reintegrating your shadow, you create two opposite symbols that you will unite in a third symbol.

Here are the steps.

1. Create the first symbol.
Find a symbol (an animal, object, mythical figure or fictitious character) that expresses what you would like to be if you were in another world and another life.

Describe its characteristics. You might describe a mountain ram, for instance, as agile, proud, noble, combative, and so on.

2. Create the second symbol.
Find a symbol (an animal, object, mythical figure or fictitious character) that expresses what you would *not* like to be if you were in another world and another life. (This second symbol corresponds to your shadow.)

Describe its characteristics. You might describe a mongrel, for instance, as dirty, helpless, starving, fearful, submissive and so forth.

3. Ask your Self — the centre of the personality that can bring the psychic poles into harmony — to synthesize these two symbols.
Stretch out your arms on either side of your body at shoulder level, looking at each of your hands in turn. Imagine that you see your first, positive symbol (for

Recovering the energies of our shadow helps us to see our mission more clearly.

example, the mountain ram) in your right hand.

Next, imagine that you see the second, negative symbol (for example, the stray dog) in your left hand.

As you take the time to bring your two hands together, ask your inner Self, your divine Centre, to integrate the two symbols and provide you with the symbol that integrates the first two.

Several participants who did this exercise faithfully succeeded in mentally seeing a third, "integrative" symbol. They are surprised to note that the new symbol often takes on a sacred or religious character. They witness the Self creating something by harmonizing the two apparently opposite symbols. The third symbol usually creates a great sense of calm, serenity and harmony within people.

✢ ✢ ✢

Gregg Levoy sees frequenting his shadow as a precious aid in discovering his mission buried in the mystery of his person: "Having free fallen into the sea of our own psyches in pursuit of dreams and passions, having climbed down the well into our own unconscious, having swapped stories with our ape-men and spent a few witching hours with our demons and daimons, we're not so scared of the dark anymore" (1997:323-324).

Recovering the energies of our shadow helps us to see our mission more clearly and access its fulfillment more easily. Whenever we honour a calling, we also tame the fear that lurks within us.

The Eagle that Thought It Was a Hen

While hiking along a mountainside, a man discovered an abandoned eagle's nest and found an egg in it. He carefully removed the egg and left it with a farmer, in the hope it could be hatched by a hen.

Not long afterward, an eaglet was born in the midst of a brood of chicks. The mother hen took care of it and raised it just like the others. One day the eaglet saw an eagle gliding through the sky. It said aloud, "When I grow up, I will fly like that bird." This drew the ridicule of the other chicks who scoffed, "You are a chicken like us!" All embarrassed, the eaglet went on acting like a chicken, pecking away at the grain.

Seeing the young eagle mature, the farmer wanted to make it fly. He picked it up in his hands and threw it into the air. But as the eaglet was convinced it could not fly, it did not open its wings. It landed awkwardly on the ground, provoking wild general laughter from the barnyard.

A little later, the farmer made a second attempt. This time, he went up onto the roof of the barn with the eaglet and threw it into the open air saying, "Fly! You are an eagle!" Timidly, the bird opened its wings and began to glide over the barnyard before finally soaring off towards the mountain.

CHAPTER 7

Seeking Your Identity

Identity and mission go hand in hand. The discovery of our mission will be hindered to the extent that we either do not know ourselves or we misunderstand ourselves. Let's remember that the word "identity" comes from the Latin *idem*, which means "the same." Identity refers to what remains the same, to that which remains stable and permanent throughout the changes and upheavals in a person's life.

Identity refers to what remains stable and permanent throughout the changes and upheavals in a person's life.

In the void created after letting go, the question that emerges, and gradually becomes more insistent, is "Who am I?" During the in-between or liminal period, an identity crisis hits; we are no longer able to define ourselves by our relationships, work, role, social standing, wealth or reputation. Deprived of these external attributes, we are left alone with ourselves to discover who we are.

A stripping away of false identities had already begun with the letting go that came with grieving and with forgiving injuries. This experience puts us in closer contact with our true selves (the Self), our deep identity that bears our mission.

Carl Jung saw "becoming your-Self" as the goal of all psychological work. He believed self-knowledge comes through dialogue between the conscious self and the unconscious Self, the spiritual centre. The Self does not allow itself to be grasped directly, but manifests itself to our consciousness through dreams, daydreams, projections, mental imagery, intuitions, etc. To perceive the Self, then, requires the work of reflecting on the clues it provides; this work allows us to discern the presence of the Self and glimpse our fundamental orientation: our mission.

We can begin to approach the Self by saying what it is not.

The following two series of exercises are designed to let you better identify the nature of the Self. The first one follows a negative approach; it consists of "disidentifying" the Self, denying what it is not. The second, which follows a symbolic approach, helps people to be attentive to the images that the Self wishes to reveal.

DISIDENTIFICATION OR LIBERATION FROM SUPERFICIAL IDENTITIES

Exercise I: Who Am I?

We have seen that the Self, a person's deeper identity, does not let itself be discovered fully by the conscious self. We can begin to approach the Self by saying what it is not. Try this disidentification exercise.

Start by listing the qualities or attributes that you recognize in yourself. Next, put these into categories that define you, going from the most exterior aspects of yourself to the most interior. The exercise is designed to bring some order to your perceptions of yourself.

In the centre of a piece of paper, write your name and then draw a circle around it. For about 10 minutes, repeat the question "Who am I?" Every time you ask the question, answer it in one or two words.

Avoid censoring your answers; let them come forth spontaneously and write them down immediately around your name. If an answer is slow in coming, write "blocked" and keep asking yourself the question. Even though you can do this exercise alone, it's preferable to do it with a person who keeps asking you, "Who are you?"

Example:

Once you've completed this exercise, put each of the words you have chosen into one of the following four categories.

Category 1
Refers to work, role, social status. Of my own responses, I would put the following words here: Canadian citizen, professor, writer, facilitator, son of Henri.

Category 2
Groups all your character traits without distinguishing between positive and negative. For example, shy, loyal, sensitive, oversensitive, affectionate, friendly.

Category 3
Encompasses the spiritual ideals called "archetypes." It represents not just your work or your social role, but the ideals that are dear to your heart. For example, in my case, priest, spiritual companion/guide, therapist, helping professional.

109

*After doing this
exercise, people
often feel freer
and more
detached*

Category 4
Relates to your personal identity. Few words fit into this category. In my case, I found only three: John, me, man. Actually, the word man does not quite do justice to what I am, because it does not take into account the feminine aspect of my person.

Once you have finished categorizing, attribute each of the qualifiers to yourself. For the first three categories, use the verb to have. Save the verb to be for the last category.

Examples:
1. I have Canadian citizenship, I have a career as a professor, I have a role as a facilitator, I have a son—father relationship with Henri, my father, etc.
2. I have friendship, I have loyalty, I have over-sensitivity, etc.
3. I have a priestly vocation, I have a mission of spiritual guidance, etc.
4. I am me; I am a man; I am John.

Ask yourself afterwards how it felt when you substituted the verb to have for the verb to be. After doing this exercise, people often feel freer and more detached; they resolve they will no longer let themselves be identified by attributes that do not describe who they really are. In this way, they learn to practise "disidentification," that is, to free themselves from their superficial identities.

Using the verb "to be" must be strictly reserved for describing your identity. Too often, this verb is improperly used, resulting in identities falsely attributed to ourselves as well as to others. For instance, one will say, wrongly, "I am an alcoholic" or "I am a liar" or "You are paranoid." It would be more accurate and liberating to say, "I have a tendency to abuse alcohol" or "Sometimes I tell lies" or "You have paranoid attitudes."

Excercise 2: Letting go of false identities

This second disidentification exercise enables us to intuitively connect with our real identity. Psychosynthesis considers this to be an exercise of primary importance. Its aim is to strip us of all that is not the essence of the Self, our true identity. It is therefore the equivalent of a letting go of the false identities we have been wearing, believing incorrectly that they were integral parts of ourselves.

If you are doing this exercise alone, it would be useful to record the following text on cassette. Being able to listen to it will free you from having to read during the exercise and will be conducive to better concentration. It is up to you to adapt it to your own personal style.

Settle into a comfortable position. Take the time to go deep inside. Close your eyes. Release the tensions in your body.

Pay attention to your breathing, your inhaling and your exhaling. This will let you enter more deeply within yourself.

You do not have to make any effort or try to understand; simply let yourself be carried by the flow of the words.

I have a body, but I am not my body.

Thousands of cells in my body die every day, while thousands of others are reborn. My body changes and ages, but I remain constant.

I am aware of having multiple sensations, but I am not my sensations; they change continually, but I remain who I am.

I have pain, but I am not my pains.

The pains change, they come and go, but I still remain the same.

I have emotions, but I am not my emotions.

I have frustrations, but I am not my frustrations.

I have fears, but I am not my fears.

I have worries, but I am not my worries.

My emotions, my frustrations, my fears, my worries come and go ceaselessly, but I remain unchangeable.

I have images and fantasies in my head, but I am neither these images nor these fantasies. These images and fantasies appear and disappear, but I remain unchanged.

I have ideas, but I am not my ideas.

They evolve endlessly, but I am still identical to myself.

I have desires and hopes, but I am neither my desires nor my hopes; they change and evolve, but I am always the same.

I have a will and intelligence, but I am neither my will nor my intelligence. These faculties develop or diminish, but I do not change.

I have a heart and I have loves, but I am neither my heart nor my loves. My heart and my loves are subject to change, but I am not subject to change, because I remain the same.

I have suffered losses in my life, I have grief to resolve, but I am neither my losses nor my grief. I will forget my losses and I will be healed from my grief, but as I pass through these changes, I will still be the same self.

I am more than my body, more than my emotions, more than my faculties, more than my loves, more than my grief.

I am . . .

Be silent now for a few moments. You will experience a feeling of peace and tranquillity. This will be a sign that you are present to your real identity, to yourself, to your Self.

At your own pace, take the time to return to your outer world and to renew contact with your surroundings.

✛ ✛ ✛

Here are some of the benefits of this disidentification exercise. If you have a migraine, for example, it is important not to identify with it as if your whole being had become a migraine. You say, therefore, "I have a migraine, but I am not my migraine." Making this distinction is conducive to better mastery over your pain. The same rule applies when it comes to the emotions. When you are disappointed, tell yourself, "I have been disappointed, but I am not my disappointment, for I am more than my disappointment." In this way you disidentify yourself from it. You thus avoid believing or giving the impression that your entire being is nothing but sadness or sorrow. This exercise lets you create within yourself a place of inner peace and freedom in response to a physical ailment or a painful situation.

Complementary exercise

Exercise 2 may be accompanied by the following ritual action. Hold in one hand a leaf-covered branch. As the exercise progresses, at intervals pull off a leaf and let it drop to the ground. At the end, all you will have left in your hand is the bare branch, the symbol of the Self. Take the time to contemplate the branch stripped of its leaves.

SYMBOLIZING YOUR AUTHENTIC SELF

Knowing your Self, your deep identity, is not achieved through logic or reason. As this knowledge is to a great extent subconscious, it is gained through dreams (including daydreams), fantasies, spontaneous intuitions, inspirations, projections and so on. All of these are messages conveyed to us by the Self in symbolic form, like rays of light piercing the night of the unconscious.

To better understand yourself, Carl Jung recommends using the active imagination to establish a dialogue between the conscious and the unconscious. The first stage of this mental process consists of making the conscious be attentive to the symbolic messages from the unconscious; in the second stage, the conscious uses these symbols, expanding on them and interpreting them. Here is an example of active imagination, in which the mind constructs a dialogue from the symbolic elements provided by the unconscious. Someone remembers having dreamt about a snake; they ask themselves what this symbolic message from their unconscious might mean. Then they undertake a dialogue with the symbol-serpent, making it talk about its needs and demands. The dreamer expresses in turn their need and makes demands on the serpent. In this way, the dreamer and the symbol-serpent establish a co-operative project. People get to know themselves by listening to and interpreting the message from the Self.

I am now going to suggest a few exercises inspired by the active imagination. You will need to allow symbolic images to rise up within you; with these images you will enter into dialogue. Bit by bit these small incursions into your imaginary world will give you access to your identity.

I am now going to suggest a few exercises inspired by the active imagination.

Exercise I: Retracing the stories that enchanted your life

The stories and tales that have charmed you since you were a child did not serve just to amuse. They have served as filters through which you have been able to get to know yourself better. They showed you ways to be, ways to behave and ways of envisaging life. They shaped your perception of what was real, contributed to how you interpreted your experiences, influenced your conduct and, later, your direction in life. The characters in these stories, as well as their missions, clearly fascinated and still fascinate you. They reveal various facets of your personality.

In a quiet place, settle down and go inside yourself. Recall a story that you found particularly exciting when you were a child. Summarize it in six to eight sentences.

Remaining in a quiet place, go inside yourself. Recall a story that you found particularly exciting during your adolescence or even in your twenties. Summarize it in a few sentences (six to eight).

Remaining in this place of quiet, recall a story that fascinated or delighted you recently (a story, a play, a film...) and that you still find fascinating or delightful. Summarize it in a few sentences (six to eight).

Alone or with two or three others, repeat the summaries of these three stories. Ask yourself the following questions:

- *With what figure, hero or heroine in the story did I identify at the different ages in my life? Did my idea of a hero or heroine evolve from one story to the next?*

- *What do these stories reveal to me about the evolution of my values, my beliefs, my relationships with others and my choices of models?*

- *What do these stories reveal to me about my psycho-spiritual evolution?*

Exercise 2: Discovering your deep values

The aim of this exercise is to help you discover the deep aspirations of your soul. To achieve this, you will observe the historical or mythical heroes/heroines for whom you have great admiration.

Name five figures (heroes, heroines, saints, spiritual leaders, inspiring men or women...) who evoke in you a feeling of admiration.

In a few words, express what it is that you find exciting in each of these people.

Ask yourself now whether this description matches the way you would describe your own desires and aspirations. Admiring a particular quality or virtue in a person is a pretty good indication that you already possess it or at least that you would like to possess it.

What you learn about yourself in this exercise will be useful when you go to define your archetype (see p. 124).

Exercise 3: Naming the symbols that represent the best of your identity

1. Based on the categories suggested, identify the two symbols that best describe your identity.

- What animal, plant, flower or tree would you like to resemble?

- What transportation vehicle would you like to be identified with?

- With what kind of landscape or scenery would you like to identify yourself?

- With what part of the body would you like to identify yourself?

  (Other possible symbols include furniture, buildings, climate, etc.)

2. Describe your two symbols in detail. See to what extent these descriptions coincide with your personality.

An interesting variation of the same exercise is called "Shadow Show." You can "play" it with three people, whom we will call A, B and C.

- A presents B with a category of symbols. A asks B to choose, for example, a kind of tree.
- B names a kind of tree, an elm, for example, and begins to describe it. C notes down the traits that B attributes to their symbol and reads the summary of the description. For example, "My elm is tall and strong; it is all alone in a field; its foliage offers hospitality to the birds; it provides shelter from the rain; sometimes it feels lonely and seeks the company of other trees"; and so on.

- Once the description of the symbol has been completed, C tells B, "You are tall and strong; you are all alone in a field; but you welcome the birds in your foliage"; and so on.
- B is asked to react to having these qualities attributed to him or her. Then, the exercise continues with B presenting to C a category of symbols and A acting as secretary.

Exercise 4: Identifying the quality or qualities that make you an original and unique person in the world

When a product is advertised, its marketers try to highlight its usefulness by comparing it to other similar products and taking care to point out its exclusive merit: "Here is a new tablet that combats heartburn faster than any other antacid." "This new soap washes whiter than white and leaves a clean, fresh fragrance; the added blue crystals make it a powerful detergent."

- If you had to present yourself in the best light to get a job, which of your qualities would you stress: intelligence, perseverance, kindness, attentiveness to people, humour, diplomacy, strength, loyalty...?
- Describe in three lines what makes you a unique being in this world.

✢ ✢ ✢

There are many other exercises to help you better discover your identity. I have chosen to present the most pertinent ones, which are designed to single out your permanent personality traits. The famous precept "Know thyself," inscribed over the portal of the Temple at Delphi, constitutes an essential tool for the process of identifying the deepest desire of your soul.

Alice is walking about in Wonderland.
Enchanted, she goes from one discovery to another.

She comes upon a crossroads.
She stops and wonders which path to take.
She doesn't know what to do.

Suddenly, she notices a hare. She runs
to meet him and says, "I have come to a
crossroads; could you tell me which
path I should take?"

The hare asks her,
"Where do you want to go?"

Shrugging her shoulders, Alice replies,
"I don't know!"

"Well then, young lady," answers the hare,
"You may take either path."

Inspired by the story *Alice in Wonderland*,
by Lewis Carroll

CHAPTER 8

Strategies for Discovering Your Mission

Your progress in self-knowledge allows you now to tackle the question "What do I want to do with my life?"

Discerning your mission is work that requires reflection, study, patience and intuition. You need to uncover the signs of this mission and to identify their points of convergence. This task is a bit like creating a mosaic. While the artist is pasting the small pieces of tile next to each other, an observer in the artist's studio cannot imagine the picture that will result. But as more and more pieces are attached, the observer can begin to see the final pattern emerging.

This chapter and the next one will suggest certain strategies aimed at helping you recognize your mission. One strategy by itself might suffice. But it is usually preferable to try several strategies. In fact, the convergence of the results will provide a more precise idea of your mission.

However, we must not delude ourselves. We do not invent a mission for ourselves; we let it be revealed to us. The strategies used to discover our mission are merely methods to facilitate reflection and meditation on inner realities such as our passions, inner calls, visions, intuitions, enthusiasms, fantasies, dreams, interests, desires, physical symptoms, and so on.

The discovery of our mission is therefore not the fruit of a purely rational endeavour, and it lacks the clarity and the precision of the rational approach. In *A Path with Heart*, Jack Kornfield reminds us that we must enter into dialogue with our heart and ask ourselves the real questions on the use of our time, energy, creativity and love. This is a work

Discerning your mission is work that requires reflection, study, patience and intuition.

When you have finished reconstructing your past, you will then be better able to recognize your soul's impulses and efforts as it strains to give birth to its mission.

of patience and interiority, undertaken in the midst of doubts, inner conflict, waxing and waning of fervour, and fear. The strategies designed to help you discover your mission will not make all your uncertainties about it evaporate or exempt you from having to take risks.

YOUR STORY: THE MATRIX OF YOUR FUTURE

The past heralds the future; the lines that you see in your past will guide you in discovering your mission. As you recall your personal story, you will be recounting the deep work of your soul and you will gradually become aware of inner calls often left unheeded or forgotten. To *remember* means to *re-member* or to "reassemble what had been dismembered or dispersed." Remembering or going back over your story allows you then to "reassemble" into a coherent whole the pieces of the puzzle of your life: scattered memories, unfulfilled desires, abandoned projects, and so on. Bit by bit, you will grasp hints of your mission which, like the stitching on a piece of cloth, appears and then disappears throughout your story.

When you have finished reconstructing your past, you will examine your passions, your tendencies, your persistent interests, your dreams – realized or abandoned. You will then be better able to recognize your soul's impulses and efforts as it strains to give birth to its mission.

Reconstructing your story

The following guidelines will help you to reconstruct your past systematically. You will need large sheets of paper and coloured markers.

- Write your name and your date of birth at the bottom of a sheet of paper.
- Go inside yourself and go back in your mind to the age of your earliest memories.
- Then, for every five-year period of your life, summarize your memories in one or two words.
- Write spontaneously from bottom to top, without trying to censor anything. Choose a specific colour for each of the following categories:

  Personal events: upbringing, schooling, games, health, happy and unhappy events, illnesses, moving, etc.

  Relational events: brothers and sisters, friends, births, deaths, friendships, broken friendships, loves, disappointments in love, groups you belonged to, etc.

  Personal accomplishments: studies, work, jobs, academic successes, products/productions/creations of any kind, failures, social responsibilities, honours, etc.

Now that you have reached your current age, continue writing spontaneously what you want to be and do.

Reflecting on the principal tendencies in your life

- Display your life review sheets on a wall.
- Choose a comfortable position and observe the panorama of your life. Ask yourself whether you have forgotten any important events. If you are doing this exercise with another person, do the review of your life together, so you can benefit from the other person's comments.
- The first part of this reflection consists of drawing up a list of the events and aspirations that tend to recur. Examine the pages that describe your story. Using a

The archetype signifies yet another way in which the psyche strives for fulfillment in relations with others.

special colour, circle the events that made the strongest impact and recurred most frequently as your life evolved (transitions, promotions, bereavements, decisions, joys, sorrows, major decisions, etc.). Number them.

• The second part consists of grouping these major events into categories. Try to connect each event with one of the archetypes described below.

Archetypes

In this context, an archetype represents the "universal type" of a particular calling or mission. The archetype signifies yet another way in which the psyche strives for fulfillment in relations with others.

You will no doubt feel that you identify more with one or a few archetypes in particular. However, this is not an exhaustive list.

• **The sage:** The guru, the man or woman of good counsel, the master, the wise old man, the crone, the wise old woman, and so on. The sage has a deep understanding of souls and communicates his or her experience with respect and consideration.

• **The leader:** The king, the political figure, the one who governs, the CEO, the orchestra conductor, and so on. The leader likes to be at the helm and have control. Leaders know the art of directing people, are good business administrators and bring their projects to completion. Efficiency is the leader's principal quality.

• **The mentor:** The companion, the spiritual mother or father, the attentive tutor or educator. The mentor encourages others, showing them the path to follow in order to grow. Mentors enjoy the successes of their disciples, guiding them with respect and discretion.

• **The protective parent:** The caregiver, the loving parent, the attentive social worker, the childcare worker, and so on. The protective parent is constantly attentive to the needs of others and ensures that their physical, psychological and spiritual comfort is secured.

• **The manager:** The authoritarian teacher, the organizer. Managers like responsibilities that call on their organizing capabilities. They dictate the rules for running things smoothly, teach how things should be done and like to take charge and bring order to a chaotic situation.

• **The healer:** The physician, the shaman, the magician, the sorceress. The healer is interested in all illnesses and various cures, whether physical, psychological or spiritual, and has a holistic approach. Normally, healers are themselves wounded healers; having gone through the healing process, they know the conditions necessary for healing.

• **The artist:** One who is fascinated by all that is beautiful; also an art critic or aesthetician; sometimes a creator; wanting to produce, they appeal to various artistic disciplines.

• **The seeker:** The scientist, the scholar, the eternal questioner. Curious and wanting to know everything, the seeker is committed to studying things from several angles.

• **The disciple:** The eternal student, the party member, the follower, the fan. The disciple ceaselessly looks for a guru, a master or a crone and is consumed by an insatiable thirst for progress under the direction of a spiritual guide.

• **The magician/sorceress:** Attracted by the marvellous, the supernatural and the extraordinary, the magician/ sorceress desires to understand both natural and supernatural laws and can manipulate them.

• **The psychologist:** Interested in the behaviour of humans and non-human animals, the psychologist seeks to discover their conscious and unconscious motives. The psychologist likes to interpret the internal dynamics of the person, especially the world of dreams.

• **The ambassador:** The negotiator, the reconciler, the intermediary, the deal-maker. Enjoying the mediator role, the ambassador is alert, perceives the needs of opposing parties and can bring those needs to coincide.

• **The wilderness man or woman:** The hunter/huntress, the trapper, the one who understands nature's secrets. Ever practical and astute, this man or woman knows how to survive even where nature is not hospitable.

• **The fool:** The court jester, the rogue, the trickster, the buffoon, the satirist, the joker. This figure makes people laugh but, in so doing, reveals something of the truths that we would rather keep hidden for fear of causing displeasure.

• **The hero or heroine:** Usually someone who takes it upon himself or herself to save their community, undaunted by having to face grave dangers. Often naive, courageous and innocent, the hero or heroine does this task generously.

• **The warrior:** The military person, the soldier, the samurai, the policeman, the defender of rights, and so on. Always ready to fight to the death for their people, their boldness is proverbial. Their frankness is brutal, for they cannot afford to indulge in illusion when faced with the danger represented by the enemy.

• **The lover:** Characterized by human warmth, openness and selflessness, the priority in the lover's life is to preserve love or friendship. (The degraded version of this archetype would be the Don Juan, the playboy, and so on.)

• **The contemplative:** The mystic, the monk, the nun, the priest and so forth. Union with God and the contemplation of spiritual realities are the focus of the contemplative's life.

• **The prophet/ess:** The clairvoyant. The prophet or prophetess recognizes signs of reality that go unnoticed by others. They interpret present signs that allow them to foretell the future. They perceive relationships between people that others are unaware of.

• **The celebrant:** Dramatic director, master of ceremonies, liturgist, liturgical presider, creator of rituals, and so on. The celebrant feels fulfilled when leading a ritual.

• **The eternal child:** The *puer aeternus* or *puella aeterna* can be recognized by their apparent innocence, kindness and dependence. They love to talk about spiritual matters, but are neither constant nor persevering in their relationships or in steady work, which requires renunciation and discipline. Agreeable company, the eternal child at first brings a certain excitement and freshness to a relationship. They also flatter and know how to manipulate others for their own ends.

Once you have grouped the major events of your life and identified the corresponding archetypes, you will have a better idea of your mission.

Once you have grouped the major events of your life and identified the corresponding archetypes, you will have a better idea of your mission. As archetypes are social realities, they can serve to describe the orientation of your gifts.

127

*It is not unusual
for the dreams of
youth to disappear
under the stress
of day-to-day
concerns.*

THE DREAMS OF ADOLESCENCE

*The unrealized dreams of our youth
always come back to haunt us.*

H. JACKSON BROWN

Adolescence is a time rich in intuitions about the future.
Writer Joseph Chilton Pearce said in his book *Evolution's End*
that adolescents have the feeling of a unique grandeur
hidden in them. It is the age of heroes and heroines.
However, they have a great fear of orienting themselves in
the wrong direction and ruining their so very precious life.
Despite the strength of their aspirations, they often feel
incapable of clearly defining their dreams of grandeur or
they become discouraged at never being able to realize them.
Disappointed, some even commit suicide. It is not unusual
for the dreams of youth to disappear under the stress of day-
to-day concerns. This is too bad, for these dreams conceal
insights into their mission.

When I was a teenager, it was clear that I wanted to be
a caregiver. What kind of caregiver? I didn't know. When I
finished my classical college studies at 19, my peers and I
decided to reveal our vocations by writing them on the
classroom blackboard. I wrote "physician." But, as I started
back to my seat, I stopped, returned to the board and added
"of souls." Little did I know at that moment that I would
spend the greater part of my life being — as a priest and a
psychologist — a physician of souls, ministering at the same
time to their physical, emotional and spiritual health.

The following questions will help you remember flashes
of intuition from your own adolescence.

- *What types of persons did you especially* not want *to become?*
- *What kinds of occupations did you find repulsive?*

- *Who were your heroes or heroines? Who were the people around you (parents, educators, neighbours, friends, etc.) who influenced you the most?*
- *What kinds of circumstances used to make you dream?*
- *What attitudes did you have towards your dreams? Did you think they were realizable or unrealizable?*

YOUR MISSION FROM THE PERSPECTIVE OF YOUR DEATH

People who have had a "near-death experience" often report that they have seen their entire life go through their mind's eye in a flash. This happened to a man who had been pronounced clinically dead. Once he was revived, he recounted his experience. A heavenly light brought him immense happiness. With all his heart, he desired to continue bathing in it. But he heard a voice enjoining him to return to earth to finish his mission of raising his children. A writer, a militant atheist, lived a similar experience. Somewhere in the "great beyond," which is where she felt she was, she met her father who, when he was alive, had been a great believer. He asked her to go back to earth to complete her spiritual evolution.

I invite you now to do an exercise described by Stephen R. Covey in his book *The Seven Habits of Highly Effective People.*

- Find a comfortable position in a calm, quiet and peaceful place.
- Imagine that you are entering a funeral home to pay your last respects to the dead body of a friend. As you cross the room, you note the fragrance of the flowers and the music of the organ. Then you meet parents, friends and acquaintances. You offer them your condolences.

- As you approach the casket, you are astonished to see your own body laid out. Then it dawns on you that you are attending your own funeral and that all these people have come to show their love and respect for you. Somewhat overcome, you take a seat in the room where the casket is. Suddenly someone brings you a booklet to help you follow the funeral service that is about to take place. There has been no mistake. It is indeed your name that is printed on the title page of the program. You even read there the names of three people you know well: a close relative, an intimate friend and a colleague from work. They will be giving the eulogies.
- Now get ready to jot down the words of praise spoken about you.
  - *What qualities does your close relative emphasize?*
  - *Your friend speaks of the quality of your human relationships. How does he describe them?*
  - *Your professional colleague recalls your qualities in the workplace. What does she say about the kind of person you are to work with?*

When you have finished your "daydream," reread your notes and ask yourself what you have learned about the mission that you are called to accomplish.

✛ ✛ ✛

You have gone back over the story of your life. You have remembered the dreams of your adolescence. You have recognized the archetypes that bring you to life. You have confirmed – as Ira Progoff taught – that the past contains the clues to the deep purposes towards which the movement of our life is trying to lead us. You have even had the courage to consider your life from the privileged perspective of the moment of your death. Congratulate yourself on the work you have completed in the process of discovering your mission.

Congratulate yourself on the work you have completed in the process of discovering your mission.

Mr. Séguin had never had much luck with his goats.

He lost them all the same way:
One fine morning, they would break loose,
go off into the mountain, and up there the wolf
would eat them. Neither their master's affection
nor their fear of the wolf could hold them back.
They were, it seemed, independent goats,
desiring freedom and the great outdoors at all costs.

ALPHONSE DAUDET

CHAPTER 9

My Passion, My Mission

WHAT DOES IT MEAN TO HAVE A PASSION FOR SOMETHING?

Passion is characterized by great emotional intensity.

Guidance counsellors and career counsellors make considerable use of various tests to uncover the talents and aptitudes of individuals. Even if these tests produce interesting results, they do not fully reveal a person's mission. What proves to be the most revealing clue to a person's orientation is their passion.

How does one define passion? *Webster's Dictionary* defines it as "a strong liking for or devotion to some activity, object or concept." It is more than a tendency, an interest or a propensity. It is characterized by great emotional intensity. Its effects on the impassioned person are many: it gives him or her a sense of living fully, even a feeling of being "worked up." It produces in such people a state of immensely feverish excitement. It drives them to concentrate all their efforts on the object of their attachment. It leads them to forget their daily routine, worries, human relationships and, at times, even their most basic biological needs.

One day, I experienced this kind of sensation: I was driving in my car, completely caught up in creating the outline of a book I wanted to write. Without realizing it, I had the accelerator practically to the floor and was flying along at a mad speed, way over the limit. Poets, under the spell of their inspiring muses, are very familiar with this kind of effervescence. Carl Jung used to call it his "daimon," a kind of inner genie who would give him a hard time until he had completed the work he was producing.

People in love are familiar examples of the impassioned person. They are sometimes so intensely

*Those who follow
their true passion
cannot "mess up"
their lives.*

absorbed by the object of their passion that they forget to
carry out their responsibilities; they might even forget where
they're going! They live only for the object of their love. The
ancient Greeks used to say of lovers that, like the gods and
goddesses such as Ares and Aphrodite, they had been struck
by a divine current of love. By contrast, certain
contemporary psychologists very unromantically compare
the passion of lovers with co-dependence or the similar
effects of drugs and the intoxication that follows. In my
view, this type of characterization does not do justice to
passionate love.

Joseph Campbell used to tell his students who were
worried about their future, "Follow your bliss." He would
encourage them to pursue the object of the passion in their
life: "If you follow your bliss, you put yourself on a kind of
track that has been there all the while, waiting for you, and
the life that you ought to be living is the one you are living.
Wherever you are – if you are following your bliss, you are
enjoying that refreshment, that life within you, all the time"
(Campbell, 1988:91). Indeed, those who follow their true
passion cannot "mess up" their lives. On the other hand,
those who turn their backs on it risk sinking into boredom.
For example, doctoral candidates who fail to choose a study
topic that excites them often stand a good chance of getting
fed up very quickly and not completing their project.

The "metapassions"

Within every surge of passion are hidden more subtle
passions or spiritual states, which I call *metapassions*. These
correspond to the aspirations of the soul. For example,
someone who has a passion for painting surely possesses the
metapassions of beauty and creativity; someone who has a

passion for cycling, the metapassion of surpassing oneself; a passion for exotic travel, the metapassion of knowing different cultures; a passion for working with immigrants and refugees, the metapassion of unconditional love. Concealed within whatever activity for which you have a soft spot lies one of your soul's spiritual aspirations.

A troubling tendency sometimes hides a spiritual aspiration which, for various reasons, has been mischannelled.

Passion and pathology

I want very much to draw your attention to what distinguishes passion from pathology. These two words share a common root, *pathos*, whose first meaning is "suffering." However, the word "passion" designates a vital and wholesome enthusiasm, while the word "pathology" designates a physical or mental illness. "Passion" refers to a burst of growth, "pathology" to an aberration. It is therefore important to avoid confusing these two realities.

The following are some examples of pathologies that are wrongly considered examples of passion: pedophiles who choose to teach children to satisfy their disordered inclination; people raised in poverty who develop an addiction to earning money; people suffering from paranoia who seek management positions solely for the purpose of controlling others. These people are following their pathology, not their passion. Choosing a particular life out of a desire to satisfy neurotic cravings necessarily leads nowhere.

On the other hand, a troubling tendency sometimes hides a spiritual aspiration which, for various reasons, has been mischannelled. Certain pathologies represent a spiritual tendency gone adrift. I think here of the character in the film *Death in Venice*, a man in late middle age who becomes infatuated with an adolescent boy. Without even

135

The following seven-stage strategy is intended to help you discover your mission by examining what arouses your passions for life.

realizing it, he falls in love with this handsome young man who, for him, symbolizes beauty, youth and a certain hermaphroditism. He is attracted by the radiance of his own soul, which he projects onto this boy: a certain asexual beauty, an eternal youthfulness and an angelic likeness.

DISCERNING YOUR MISSION BY EXAMINING YOUR PASSION

In search of what excites you

I invite you now to ask yourself some questions on what constitutes your passion. Each of your answers will provide a clue as to what your mission might be.

- *What makes you feel you are really living, not just surviving?*
- *What hobby or leisure pursuit do you find really exciting?*
- *What section do you immediately go to when you enter a bookstore?*
- *What television or radio programs do you find fascinating?*
- *What topics of conversation do you find most stimulating?*

The following seven-stage strategy is intended to help you discover your mission by examining what arouses your passions for life.

Stage I: List the most fulfilling activities in your life

- Identify three experiences where you felt totally fulfilled, enthusiastic and happy.
- Describe them as if you were living them, using verbs in the present tense.
- Reread your descriptions. Circle the words that you consider important, especially the verbs. Feel free to add clarifications or clarifying details.
- Identify the common elements of the three experiences:

words, feelings, actions, contexts, and so on. Single out the principal orientations and recurring themes. These are important elements of your mission.
• Write a synthesis of your discoveries. Using the key words and important expressions, write a sentence that will become a first draft of your mission statement.

Stage 2: First draft of your mission statement

Reread your mission statement.
• *Does it accurately describe the deep orientation of your soul?* Make any changes needed to make it clearer and more precise.
• *Is it succinct? Have you kept it to just one or two lines?*
• *Does it include action verbs?*
• *Is it expressed in positive terms?*

Stage 3: Checking the authenticity of your mission statement

• Single out four or five of your qualities that justify or confirm your mission statement. Example: If my mission is to listen to others, I will have to be patient, empathetic, frank, and accept them unconditionally.
• Make two columns. Put these qualities in the left column; next to each one, in the right column, describe an actual event that confirms that you possess the quality you listed.

Qualities for your mission	Verification (events showing that you actually possess these qualities)
1)	
2)	
3)	
4)	
5)	

Stage 4: Cross-checking the accuracy of your mission statement

• For each quality, think of an occasion when you should have used it, but didn't. For example, "Quality: empathy – I would have liked to spend time listening attentively to a neighbour in need, but was not able to because I had too much work."

• For each event, answer the following questions:
  — *What feelings did you experience?*
  — *How do you feel when your actions do not bring into play this quality that is so important in the framework of your mission?*

That you failed to practise this quality when it was important to do so strengthens the notion that it has a major role in your mission. If you experienced feelings of uneasiness or frustration, they further confirm the importance of this quality for your mission.

First quality: _____

Situation where applying this *My reaction to this omission*
quality would have been important

Second quality: _____

Situation where applying this *My reaction to this omission*
quality would have been important

Third quality: _____

Situation where applying this *My reaction to this omission*
quality would have been important

Fourth quality: _____

Situation where applying this   *My reaction to this omission*
quality would have been important

Fifth quality: _____

Situation where applying this   *My reaction to this omission*
quality would have been important

Stage 5: Second tentative mission statement and the qualities needed to carry it out

Rewrite your mission statement as well as the qualities it involves:

• Proceed now to a more comprehensive cross-check of the authenticity of your statement. Ask yourself, "What would happen to my life if I did not carry out my mission statement?"
• For a few moments, imagine a situation where you could not realize your mission as described in your statement. Identify your reactions as well as the feelings that arise in you.
• What is really going on inside you? Does this cross-check frighten you?

Stage 6: Third tentative mission statement – your mission situated in its context

• In exactly what context(s) do you expect to carry out your mission?
(Examples: education, family, media, health, the elderly, poverty, immigration, alcoholism and drug addiction, adolescents, church, spirituality, palliative care, literacy, sexuality, fine arts, sports…)

Your statement must make clear that you have assumed responsibility for your mission and that it lies within your power to carry it out.

• Now indicate the context you have chosen and add it to your second mission statement.

Stage 7: Conditions for ensuring that your statement is more authentic

• You will no doubt want to improve this mission statement still further. To help you do so, read the conditions that will make your statement more faithful, concrete and effective.

• When you read your mission statement aloud, you should normally feel elated, inspired and attracted by it. If it does not awaken enthusiasm in you or does not call upon your talents and qualities, modify the statement to make it more exciting and appealing.

Your mission statement must be able to encompass succinctly the whole of your life's activities. Look, for example, at how Jesus Christ stated his mission: "I came that they may have life and have it abundantly" (John 10:10). He used this statement as his constant motivation in all areas of his life. It would be difficult to find a single moment where it was not his point of reference.

Your statement must make clear that you have assumed responsibility for your mission and that it lies within your power to carry it out. What would you think of a mission worded this way: "I want solely to make my children happy"? Realizing such a mission would be impossible. In fact, we cannot create happiness for others. A suitable formulation might be something like this: "My mission is to create, foster and maintain a family and learning environment that is peaceful, conducive to fulfillment and open to change, in a way that will encourage my children's personal growth."

To be acceptable, a mission statement should be compatible with that of your employer or of the institution you belong to. Thus, for example, a priest's mission could read: "My mission is to be a witness to God's love through my conduct, my prayer, my speech and my liturgical celebrations." This mission fits easily within the Church's main mission, to work for the greater glory of God and the salvation of humanity.

In certain cases, it may turn out to be impossible to reconcile one's mission with that of one's employer. I am thinking here of the caregiver who refused to follow the instructions of his superiors with respect to the treatment of sexual abuse offenders. He reproached his superiors for their ineffectual, humiliating and disrespectful way of dealing with the offenders. Rather than betray his mission of caregiver as he envisioned it, he chose to resign and start up his own consulting business, even though it meant a significant drop in salary and employment benefits.

It should be made clear that your mission statement is not carved in stone. As you actualize your mission, you will need to modify your statement. It will become even more precise and will have to take into account your mission's future scope. Accomplishing your mission is a bit like clearing a path through the bush: your only option is to create it as you go.

Your mission statement is not carved in stone.

Sample mission statements

- My mission consists of helping people find a reason for living, encouraging them to continue their search and supporting them in their efforts by designing and offering workshops.
- I would like to work on my own physical, emotional and

spiritual growth so I can better help others enjoy a richer and more fulfilling life.

- My mission consists of exploring and perfecting new educational methods that will contribute to more effective and more enriching ways of teaching.

- My mission is to create places where people learn to express their artistic talents.

- Rooted in the conviction that peace is always possible, my mission consists of helping people resolve their conflicts, forgive themselves and one another, and learn to live in harmony.

- My mission is to discover and perfect new psychological and spiritual strategies that will enable individuals in a university setting to become personally fulfilled.

- I would like to be an agent of change in the Church and in society through writing and public speaking.

- I sense I am being called to become a communicator, serving as intermediary between various cultures to foster knowledge, respect and exchange between people of diverse cultural backgrounds.

- I am discovering my mission in being a spiritual companion to people, in a way that enables them to discover their own spirituality and helps them to live it.

✢ ✢ ✢

To conclude this chapter, I offer a story told to me by the chaplain of a long-term care facility. A disabled woman, paralyzed and in a wheelchair, shared with the chaplain the story of how she had discovered her mission. She had been angry with life because she was finding her existence totally useless. However, after assisting at the celebration of the sacrament of the sick at her dying mother's bedside, she let go of all the resentments she had built up against her mother and forgave her. Delivered from this burden she had been carrying, she now felt called to console others around her who looked dejected or depressed. This is how she described to the chaplain her newly discovered mission: to bring a smile to the faces of people who are sad. When she would meet a person who appeared sullen or downcast, she would always manage to clown about or tell a joke in a way that would cheer them up. According to the chaplain, that woman has been faithful to her mission ever since.

Another way of seeing freedom began
to make its way into my consciousness,
far below the surface. It was the freedom
to follow my life project, making all
the commitments I could honour.
And, at the same time, I would allow the
creative forces of my life to invade me
without any control on my part, without
any effort by me to "make it work."
As I would learn over time, this is a
much more powerful way of functioning
than trying to control everything.

JOSEPH JAWORSKI

There is a basic truth about any creative act
or initiative a person undertakes and it is this:
from the moment one becomes committed to it with
conviction, Providence becomes an ally.

JOHANN WOLFGANG GOETHE

CHAPTER 10

How the Universe Calls You

So far, I have been focusing on seeking and discovering our mission from the point of view of the person doing the seeking and the discovering. It is time now to envisage mission by taking into account the participation of the universe.

Indeed, the longings of the soul and the callings of the universe correspond mysteriously to one another. Some people discover their mission when they are exposed to situations of want, such as extreme poverty, inadequate education or glaring deprivation, or when they witness situations crying out for help – like a relationship that has fallen apart or some other kind of crisis. From their initial reaction of being emotionally upset, they move on to actively address the need. Others find their mission when they learn of certain possibilities being offered to them: an unexpected invitation to stretch their comfort zone, a surprise promotion, inspiration for a useful invention, the opportunity for a good business deal, a chance conversation that opens up new horizons, an attractive job offer, and so on.

We will develop three reflections here on how the universe calls us. First, we will examine ourselves to see whether we have an optimistic or pessimistic image of the world; second, we will ask ourselves to what extent we are aware of the phenomenon of synchronicity; finally, we will look at the relevance of prophetic messages about our mission from those around us.

The longings of the soul and the callings of the universe correspond mysteriously to one another.

The problem is not so much whether life is giving us a chance at success and fulfillment, but whether we are ready to respond to life's invitations

My eye on the universe: optimistic or pessimistic?
The metaphor may be the most effective tool human beings possess. Its virtual reality holds magical power, and it is a method of creation that God seems to have left behind in us at the time of our creation.

JOSÉ ORTEGA Y GASSET

How we view the universe affects our ability to discover our mission either favourably or unfavourably. Why can certain people perceive and seize upon the chances of success that are offered to them while others don't even see them? Reality is rich with possibilities, bursting with opportunities for realizing ourselves and our dreams. The problem is not so much whether life is giving us a chance at success and fulfillment, but whether we are ready to respond to life's invitations. It is becoming increasingly clear that people's behaviour depends on their understanding of the world. If they see it as a friendly reality, full of resources, they will not fear to act boldly. If, on the other hand, they perceive it as hostile and threatening, they will tend to avoid taking risks and withdraw.

HOW METAPHORS FILTER YOUR PERCEPTIONS

Linguists stress the importance of metaphors in the representation of the real. Metaphors are much more than simple stylistic devices: they condition our perception and interpretation of the world, thus influencing our behaviour. If you examine closely the metaphors people use, you can tell whether they perceive the world as a friendly or a hostile place. For example, "life is a garden to be cultivated" suggests an optimistic and enthusiastic attitude to life. In contrast, "life is a minefield" speaks of distrust and will paralyze any initiative involving risk.

Here are other examples of emotional reactions evoked by opposite sets of metaphors. Affirmations like "life is about entering the spirit of the game," "life only asks you to sing the song in your heart," "the world is a rich and varied bouquet offered to each one of us," "everyone is potentially willing to co-operate," "reality is bursting with resources ready to be tapped" and "success begins with a dream" evoke in us a renewed spirit of enthusiasm, a taste for daring, the desire to benefit from opportunities that present themselves. On the other hand, when someone says "the world is a rough sea tossing us about," "life is the pits," "everyone's just out to get you," "the world is a time-bomb waiting to explode," "I wasn't born under a lucky star" or "life is a train passing me by," we cannot help but sense uneasiness, a fear of adventure and the need for self-protection.

The metaphors we use to describe life or the world are all filters that colour reality for better or for worse.

The metaphors we use to describe life or the world are all filters that colour reality for better or for worse. They magnify or shrink reality; they herald opportunity or danger; they evoke boldness or fear.

Transforming your metaphors

Are you surprised to find yourself using limiting and constraining metaphors? If so, all is not lost. You still can alter your metaphors to your advantage; they are not carved in stone. They are the result of unhappy experiences that you have turned into absolutes and from which you tend to generalize. For example, after repeatedly failing in his studies, one of my clients stated with conviction, "For me, studying is

Recently I suggested to one of my students that she transform her metaphors.

just an unscalable mountain; it's like banging my head against a big rock." First, I got him to see that these metaphors did not express the whole of his experience. His studies could also be compared to "a mountain holding joy-filled surprises along the climb" and that any kind of learning is "an interesting and challenging adventure." I had him engrave the image of the mountain in his mind and he described to me, step by step, his climb and the numerous happy discoveries he had made along the way. Not long afterwards, he confided that he was finding his studies easier and that, for the first time, he had read a book from cover to cover.

Recently I suggested to one of my students that she transform her metaphors. She had been complaining that her life was far too busy. She felt "bogged down by her commitments, weighed down by her burdens." Knowing that she loved to dance, I advised her to imagine life as a dance. Skeptical at first, she eventually agreed to try it. She wondered what form of dance would best represent her hectic life. Spontaneously, she came up with rock 'n' roll. Since her discovery, her attitude has changed: she carries out her numerous tasks to the lively beat of rock 'n' roll music.

Transforming your metaphors into images of growth and fulfillment

Here is a strategy aimed at replacing your defeatist perceptions of life with new ones that are filled with promise. It lets you perceive your mission optimistically and enables you to benefit from all the opportunities you are given to accomplish it.

• Think of all the metaphors that you hold to be true about life and the world. Write three or four of them down on a sheet of paper.

• Study each metaphor, asking yourself the following questions:

— What does this metaphor represent for me?

— What emotional reactions does it provoke in me?

Example. If you have stated that "life is one long struggle" or that "life is sacred," ask yourself what effect this conviction produces on your relationships and on your attitude towards life.

Are your metaphors conducive to your development?

• Transform your pessimistic metaphors.

Are you satisfied with the impact of your metaphors on your life? Are they conducive to your development? If not, here is what you can do to alter them and make them more positive. Begin by seeing that your belief is relative. If, for example, life appears to you as "a battlefield" or "a valley of tears," acknowledge that, although it does at times involve competition and disappointment, life is also "an interesting game" or "continuous negotiation" and that, although it has its times of sorrow, it is on the whole "a grace," "gift," "a dance."

• Replace the metaphors that describe your mission.

Some people want to describe their mission using a metaphor. If you want to do this, answer the following questions using metaphors:

— What is your idea of a perfect world? What would be your ideal in such a world? Let images that correspond to your aspirations and values form in your mind. Even if the image that appears at first seems exaggerated or unrealistic, don't hesitate to hold on to it. It will stimulate and comfort you as you accomplish your mission.

To help you create your own metaphors, here are a few illustrations:

There is a mysterious correspondence between the movements of the soul and the callings of the universe.

— The world is a huge laboratory where I let myself learn by trial and error.
— Life is a dance, sometimes slow and sometimes fast.
— The world is a vast, fertile field to be sown and harvested.
— Life is a game where everyone wins.
— The world is a sacred trust.
— The universe is a mysterious symphony.

• Transcribe onto signs the metaphors that you have just created and place them where you can see them easily so that they become solidly anchored in you. As you look at them day after day, your way of seeing, hearing and experiencing reality will be transformed.

SYNCHRONICITY: PAYING ATTENTION TO THE FORTUITOUS INVITATIONS OF THE UNIVERSE

There is a mysterious correspondence between the movements of the soul and the callings of the universe. The Swiss psychoanalyst Carl Jung was the first to use the term *synchronicity* to designate this phenomenon. He defined it as a correlation between what is happening in people's inner life and what is happening outside them. This correspondence can be observed but is difficult to explain. The laws of synchronicity are neither a matter of chance nor of linear cause and effect. They therefore remain a mystery, but this does not make them less real. Due consideration of this phenomenon seems to point to an orchestration of events by a superior intelligence that some people call Providence.

One day, as Jung was about to interpret a client's dream about a beetle, a specimen of the insect crashed into the window of the office. Jung picked up the insect and presented it to his client, saying, "Here is your beetle!" In his opinion, a kind of affinity had been established between the client's dream and the universe.

Incidents that may appear insignificant on the surface sometimes hold clues about the direction of our mission. Gregg Levoy, author of *Callings*, claims to have been most intrigued to encounter the Queen of Hearts very frequently, over a short period of time, when he was playing cards. Only later did he understand that he needed to shed an attitude that was too masculine and rational in his writing. To nourish his inspiration as a writer, he needed to be more in touch with his *anima*, his feminine side, particularly by paying attention to his sensitive and emotional side. That was the message he thought the Queen of Hearts wanted him to hear.

Some students told me how one day they were wondering whether or not they should stage a strike to change the unjust conditions in which they found themselves. Just at that moment, they heard revolutionary chanting on the radio, and so decided to go on strike.

No doubt you, too, have had such experiences, just when you were questioning your plans, feelings, desires, and direction. Reality often gives us signs of the mission that awaits us, but unfortunately, we are not always ready to recognize them. We are not always prepared to tune in to the right frequency. When you are wondering about your mission, be more attentive to the incidents or events that upset or disturb the normal course of your life: an illness, an unexpected visit, a bizarre incident, a chance conversation, a repeated mistake, a recurring dream, the appearance of unusual objects or strange animals, and so forth.

The challenge of synchronicity is determining the correct

Reality often gives us signs of the mission that awaits us, but unfortunately, we are not always ready to recognize them.

151

Happy are those who have the good fortune to encounter "prophets of encouragement" who recognize in them the signs of their mission.

meaning or interpretation of such incidents or events. We must resist the temptation to explain them too literally or to overreact to the slightest unusual happening. If an incident has an important message for your mission, it will recur and become more insistent.

Messages from those around you

As we have already seen, the projections made by those who play an important role in your life can be a heavy burden to carry. Some parents wish that their child would carry out the mission that they had envisaged for themselves but missed in their lives; a good many children have thus been led to follow a path that was not theirs. Others were subjected to the influence of "prophets of doom" who discouraged them from persevering in the search for and pursuit of their mission. I remember a French professor of mine playing the prophet and predicting, "You'll never be able to write!" And what should I make of the editor who, after reading the original French version of my manuscript *How to Love Again*, advised me patronizingly, "You know, you really should give up this writing project; there would just be too much work involved in correcting your manuscript"? Yet today 165,000 copies of that book are in print!

On the other hand, happy are those who have the good fortune to encounter "prophets of encouragement" who recognize in them the signs of their mission. Jesus Christ was such a prophet. Often, he would point out to someone what their mission was, right from their first meeting. Indeed, he said to Peter, "I will make you a fisher of people!"

One of the chapters in James Hillman's book *The Soul's Code* is entitled *"Esse est Percipi:* To Be Is to Be Perceived." In this chapter, Hillman gives several examples of people who became what certain prophets or mentors who, able to see beyond the surface, had perceived in them. Franklin Roosevelt saw in Lyndon Johnson a future president of the United States. George Washington selected Alexander Hamilton, an inexperienced young soldier whom he did not know, as his principal aide-de-camp. Professor William James believed in the abilities of a somewhat neurotic young Jewish woman named Gertrude Stein. Sure of his intuition, he gave her a passing grade on an exam that she had actually failed. He continued to give her his constant assistance and even recommended her for medical studies at John Hopkins University. She eventually became a well-known American writer. A more contemporary example of this phenomenon would be René Angelil's discovery, in a 13-year-old girl, of the greatest pop singer to ever come from Quebec, Céline Dion.

Certain teachers can glimpse a brilliant future for individuals in whom others have seen only ordinary talent or even a lack of talent.

We encounter this type of intuition in certain teachers, professors, mentors, sports coaches, and "head hunters" in sports and in the arts. They can glimpse a brilliant future for individuals in whom others have seen only ordinary talent or even a lack of talent.

Here are a few questions to help stimulate your reflection on your mission.

— *Have you met these prophets of encouragement?*
— *What did you learn from them about your life project?*
— *How did you react to their prophecy about you?*
— *Do you believe their opinion confirmed your own intuition about your mission?*

PART FOUR

The New Beginning

The facilitator of a group asked
the participants to go out into a field
and pick four-leaf clovers.

After a few hours of intense searching,
no one except one young woman had been able to find a
single one.
She returned with a
fistful of lucky clovers which she distributed
to the other members of the group.

They asked her what secret
had allowed her to find so many.

She answered, "It's simple; I imagined
a four-leaf clover; all I had to do after that
was go and spot them and pick them."

CHAPTER 11

Imagining in Detail the Reality of Your Mission

Accordingto William Bridges, after the letting go and the in-between period or liminal phase, we re-enter the community in a new way to affirm our mission. Characteristically, at this stage we make a definite commitment to a new direction.

If this new stage constitutes a clear step forward, we can be sure that we are not alone in going through it. On this point, H.H. Murray claims that, from the moment we become fully engaged in our mission, Providence engages itself on our side: all kinds of unforeseeable and unanticipated events take place – incidents, fortuitous encounters, material assistance, anything that contributes to our mission being realized once we have made a firm decision. Indeed, when we actively pursue our mission, the saying "I do my best and God does the rest" applies totally.

One thing I do not want to do is leave you with the impression that everything will be easy from here on in. Therefore, it is important to examine the kinds of resistance that are inherent in this stage, for you will have to deal with them. Then we will look at how to describe your mission in detail and affirm your ideal vision of it.

It is important to examine the kinds of resistance that are inherent in this stage, for you will have to deal with them.

TYPES OF RESISTANCE TO ENGAGEMENT

Once you've written your mission statement, you will have made considerable progress in the discovery of your mission. However, it often happens that the further you advance, the more objections you think of. The closer you get to your goal, the more insidious and persistent these objections will become. Just when you're about to move into action,

Initial resistance consists of believing that we should be quite sure of our mission before launching into it.

resistance is at its strongest. This is an indication that you are about to strike gold.

Refusing to commit to your mission before being certain that it's the right one

Initial resistance consists of believing that we should be quite sure of our mission before launching into it. Some people don't dare to venture into their mission unless they are sure that it's the right one. They undergo every available psychological test imaginable; they try every avenue suggested; they weigh all the possibilities of success and failure; they analyze their abilities and talents from every angle. But this is wasted effort, for they will never get absolute assurance that they're on the right track. In this regard, we must be content with relative certainty and be willing to take calculated risks.

Some people begin to doubt whether their mission statement is accurate, asking themselves, "Did I make a mistake? Was I kidding myself?" They need to set aside such doubts and worries. The advantage of a mission statement is that it describes a direction that is more precise than what you had before. Remember that you cannot go wrong if you commit yourself to a path that you are passionate about. And your mission statement is not carved in stone. You can always correct it and improve it.

Fear of acquiring too much power

Can we be afraid to succeed in life? Strange as that may seem, many of us are forced to admit this to be the case. We feel dizzy the minute we start to succeed in our mission, intimidated by finding ourselves under the critical eye of the gallery.

Those who are victims of the Jonah complex would prefer to let their potential lie dormant. That will spare them the anxiety of having to face humiliation, envy, criticism, rivalry and the risk of failure. And so they practise avoidance techniques: they stay in the shadows; they keep their aspirations modest and purposely appear stupid or incapable; they have recourse to all sorts of pretexts to justify their inaction.

Others, in a kind of self-sabotage, are tempted to give up as soon as they see that their mission may succeed. They fear acquiring new power that will demand too much of them. Their shadow keeps their ardent desire for power repressed, and they are constantly protecting themselves against anxiety attacks from that facet of their shadow.

A number of us are afraid to use our imaginations to envision the future.

Fear of imagining the future

A number of us are afraid to use our imaginations to envision the future. Why this reticence? I thought the *Oxford Thesaurus* might shed some light on this question if I looked up the synonyms for the word *vision*. I was astonished that so many of the words suggested had negative connotations: "dream, hallucination, chimera, optical illusion, mirage, illusion, delusion, figment of the imagination." Indeed, the word *imagination* itself tends to be suspect. We say, "It's just your imagination," or "Don't get carried away by your imagination," or "Now, don't start imagining things." However, while the thesaurus did include synonyms like "unreality" and "phantom" for imagination, it also gave "creative power, creativity, inspiration, insight, inventiveness, originality, resourcefulness, ingenuity and enterprise." Unless you allow yourself to imagine and be creative, you limit your ability to create and plan projects for the future.

Some people tend to throw themselves headlong into pursuing their new direction.

Writers like Joseph Conrad have gone so far as to say that it is only in the human imagination that truth has real existence! Conrad called imagination the supreme teacher of art and of life. Just think of expressions like "Follow your dream" or "The sky's the limit." It is extremely important to be attentive to the mental images you carry, for they have the power to let you see life as a source of abundance or, conversely, as nothing but problems.

Other kinds of resistance

On the other hand, some people tend to throw themselves headlong into pursuing their new direction. Completely excited, they skip the stages of preparation and growth. There is just no stopping them, they are so gung-ho. A woman who had just discovered her talent for poetry was absolutely determined that her first poems would be published by a well-known publishing house!

Then there are those who are tempted to look back. Feeling nostalgic for the past, they delight in recalling their past successes. They resemble the people of Israel who, although they had been freed from slavery, began to wish they had the security of Egypt again.

Other people let themselves be deterred and discouraged by the slightest negative remark from people around them. Super-sensitive to the reactions of family, friends or acquaintances, they prefer to change direction rather than tolerate the discomfort of criticism.

Detailed description of your mission

To overcome these obstacles, it is good to proceed systematically. At first, the mission statement describes an ideal in broad terms, vaguely and abstractly. It is now time to reformulate it in a more concrete, contextualized way. This is the aim of the "affirmation" approach. It consists of coming up with an idea of the details of your mission that is as precise as possible and then appealing to your creative imagination, considering that it has already actualized.

In his book *Everyday Miracles: The Inner Art of Manifestation*, David Spangler describes the importance of this creative function: "For human beings, imagination is the womb of reality. All that exists for us in our human world began in someone's imagination" (1996:148). Never underestimate the power of the creative imagination: it programs both the success and the failure of what we undertake. The affirmation presupposes that you consider reality as a place where success and possibilities reside. On the other hand, if you subscribe to ideas of failure and humiliation, you thereby attract failure and humiliation.

Here's how you can create for yourself a strong and entrancing vision of your mission by using the "affirmation" method.

Never underestimate the power of the creative imagination: it programs both the success and the failure of what we undertake.

USING THE "AFFIRMATION" APPROACH

The advantage of this approach is that it can motivate you strongly to achieve the goal you seek. Setting out your mission in detail puts you on the trail of opportunities that will help you realize it; you will therefore be in a better position to take advantage of those opportunities. The "affirmation" echoes the method of prayer that Jesus taught: "So I tell you, whatever you ask for in prayer, believe that you have received it, and it will be yours" (Mark 11:24).

In the first step, you want your "affirmation" to provide you with a detailed vision of your mission which, once you have expressed it, you will call your "ideal vision." In the second step, you let your "affirmation" invite you to imagine this vision fully realized.

I. Write down the ideal vision of your mission

A few concrete examples will illustrate, first of all, what I mean by the "ideal vision" of a mission.

• I had expressed my mission statement as follows: "To communicate knowledge that empowers people to help themselves, heal themselves and grow psychologically and spiritually."

Compare this with the ideal vision of what I had envisaged doing at a certain point in my life: "I popularize psychological and spiritual knowledge aimed at progressively wider audiences. In addition to my work as a professor, I accept invitations to give talks, hold workshops and do interviews for the various media. I give priority to training sessions for 'trainers': teachers/professors, professionals, priests, parents, and so forth. I write popular books that will help people deal with their grief, learn to forgive and develop greater self-esteem."

• Some ideal visions are even more precise. One person described his mission in this way: "I want to attain financial independence quite early on in my life so that I can then devote myself to an activity I'm passionate about." His ideal vision looked like this: "I earn my first million dollars by age 30. I devote myself to my passion: wine tasting. I become an expert in enology (the science that deals with wine and wine-making). I travel all over the world to give workshops and seminars for wine lovers."

• Then there was the radio broadcaster who also pictured his mission very concretely: "I want to work independently, serving the public in a food-related activity." His ideal vision of that mission? Being his own boss, working with members of his family in the restaurant business; his customers are satisfied. His ideal vision of his mission became a reality when he became the owner of a smoked-fish shop. As anticipated, it became a family business. The products were displayed on a stand adjoining the shop. I later saw him in a television report, in the midst of his family, proudly offering his smoked salmon and trout to his customers.

Begin by drawing up a list of what you need to make your mission happen

Establishing more concrete intermediate goals

Your ideal vision can be much too general and remote to have any hold over your imagination. You will need to subdivide it into small, ideal visions describing intermediate goals.

Begin by drawing up a list of what you need to make your mission happen: human resources and materials; practical, academic and social skills; moral qualities like perseverance, calm, enthusiasm; generosity towards others; the ability to meditate; and so on. Next, prioritize these visions or goals.

Go back to my example of the ideal vision of my mission: "I popularize psychological and spiritual knowledge for progressively wider audiences...." To successfully educate others through my speaking and writing, I needed to be in good health. Therefore, after I suffered a mild stroke, my short-term vision of my mission was to recover my health by every means at my disposal.

Here were my priorities:
- First intermediate goal: *Improve my health.*
- Second intermediate goal: *Improve my oral and written expression.*
- Third intermediate goal: *Agree to speak to progressively larger audiences.*

Express your ideal vision as if you had already achieved it.

Writing an effective ideal vision

Follow these few rules when you write your ideal vision, and you'll make it both attractive and entrancing.

• Your ideal vision must be positive.

— Say: *I have the energy, the drive and the stamina to speak in public and to write for a few hours a day.*

— Don't say: *I am not tired of speaking and writing.* Such a formulation will do nothing to stimulate your imagination and will often produce the opposite of the desired effect.

• Make sure you, not someone else, can realize the content of your ideal vision.

— Say: *I eat a healthy diet; I get enough rest to be able to do my work; I take vitamin supplements as well as the medication prescribed by my doctor.*

— Don't say: *I want the doctor to cure me and get me back into good shape physically.*

• Express your ideal vision as if you had already achieved it.

— Say: *I feel full of energy; I am enjoying better health; I am eating properly; I am exercising regularly; etc.*

— Don't say: *I should eat better; I should get physical exercise; etc.* Avoid using the future or the conditional tense; human nature is such that your vision will just end up gathering dust on the shelf and you will keep on postponing achieving it.

• For your vision to maintain its hold over your imagination, it's important that it describe in detail the goal to be realized. Don't omit physical awareness, movements, colours, smells, sounds, tactile sensations and so forth. This will help you be mentally convinced that you are dealing with a concrete goal to be pursued immediately. Your vision thus constitutes a highly motivating "mental picture."

— Say: I take a 45-minute nature walk in the morning. I eat healthy foods, fresh fruits and vegetables; I take my vitamins regularly; I drink four to eight glasses of water a day; etc.
— Keep it concrete; avoid talking in the abstract: I exercise; I eat better…
If you feel uncomfortable or doubtful when you read your ideal vision, then it is not sufficiently in tune with your overall personality. In psychological jargon, we'd say that it doesn't correspond to the ecology of your person. In that case, try to improve or change it right away.

If you feel uncomfortable or doubtful when you read your ideal vision, then it is not sufficiently in tune with your overall personality.

2. "Affirm" realization of the ideal vision of your mission
Once you've created your ideal vision in a way that will stimulate your imagination, you still need to "affirm" its realization. Use one of the following strategies as a guide.

These two strategies are aimed at maintaining the creative tension necessary to realize your ideal vision. It is up to you to choose the one that will work best for you.

I. Visualizing *What Could Be (your ideal vision)*
Train yourself to visualize What Could Be (your ideal vision).

Find a comfortable position and relax as you listen to the sounds you hear around you. This will allow you to enter more deeply within yourself.

Look around and observe the colours, shapes and contrasts of light and shadow. This too will let you go even more deeply into yourself.

Become aware of your breathing: breathe in, breathe out. See which one is longer … This exercise will also take you deeper into yourself.

Feel yourself gradually being bathed in a soft, spiritual light.
Imagine that you have realized the goal of your ideal vision: you have succeeded in realizing your mission as you had pictured it.

Repeat this meditation once a day.

You become aware that your outlook on the world, on events, on people and on yourself has changed.

You see your new life project in detail and you're proud of it.

Create for yourself a vivid colour image of your new situation.

Listen to the new dialogue playing inside your head.

Listen to all the people talking about your success.

Listen to the comments people around you have been making ever since you reached your goal.

Congratulate yourself!

Taste the joy, the satisfaction and the happiness of seeing your mission accomplished.

Allow yourself to experience true pride in your accomplishments and your success.

At the end of your meditation, pray in thanksgiving to God or to the Providence that has granted you such success.

Then, slowly and at your own pace, return to the world around you, bringing with you the feelings of joy, satisfaction and happiness that you have just experienced.

Take another moment of silence and feel totally fulfilled and confident in the face of life's new challenges.

Don't talk to anyone about your meditation. It's your secret. Continue to live and go about your business as if nothing had happened.

Repeat this meditation once a day, in the morning or evening, in a calm and quiet place. This will enable you to perceive and seize opportunities that will help you achieve your mission. You will get involved in the activities necessary to accomplish your life's dream. You will get there without great effort, assured that Providence or the universe is collaborating in carrying out your life project.

2. *What Is Now* (your current situation) compared to *What Could Be* (your ideal vision)
In *The Path: Creating Your Mission Statement for Work and for Life,* Laurie Beth Jones suggests an interesting visualization exercise that requires some skillful mental gymnastics. You need to simultaneously sustain in your mind two superimposed images, as sometimes seen on a television screen.

The first image portrays your current situation; the second is that of your ideal vision. All great artists have this faculty of being able to see their completed masterpiece in their mind's eye, done in their own medium; painters project it onto a blank canvas; sculptors detect it in the block of stone; musicians hear it before they translate it into a score.

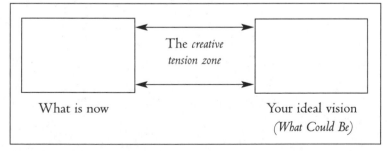

The *creative* tension zone

What is now

Your ideal vision
(*What Could Be*)

Your vision of What Could Be will create such enthusiasm that it will overcome any inertia or insecurity that you may feel in the face of the unknown.

At first, the necessary stress of seeing the gap between your current situation and the new vision of your mission will cause you some tension. Try to sustain the *creative tension* between what already exists and what will happen once your mission has been carried out.

Using this strategy will keep you from sliding back into your comfortable old routine – your ineffective and boring routine. Your vision of *What Could Be* will create such enthusiasm that it will overcome any inertia or insecurity that you may feel in the face of the unknown.

When I began learning Neuro-Linguistic Programming (NLP) in psychotherapy, I was really excited about how effective this method was. In the training workshops, I could observe for myself the rapid and lasting changes that this approach produced in clients. But even though I was so taken by this method, I did not manage to use it in my own practice.

It happened that at the end of a four-day training session, John Grinder, one of the founders of NLP, suggested an exercise that could help us apply the knowledge we had gained during the workshop. First, he put us in a kind of trance, then he had us visualize mentally our office and future clients with whom we would use only NLP strategies.

The next morning, I spontaneously applied NLP strategies with my first client. Since that time, I have never hesitated in the least to use this approach. To my great amazement, the visualization suggested by John Grinder had made me let go of my old habits. I experienced the great power that an ideal vision can have in bringing about a successful future.

A tourist visiting a leprosarium
was taking photos of a nun
dressing a patient's wound.
When he had finished, he exclaimed,
"For all the money in the world,
I would never do this kind of work!"
The nun answered,
"You're right, neither would I."

CHAPTER 12

Your Mission in Action

To push a rocket beyond earth's gravity requires a colossal force. But once in orbit, the law of inertia ensures it will keep moving unassisted. In a parallel manner, taking those first steps towards carrying out your life project requires a great deal of energy and courage. While you are exploring your mission, you will experience some critical moments when the temptation to give up will become an obsession. A thousand questions will dance around in your head: "What if I'm making a mistake? What if all the time, resources and effort I'm investing are for nothing? Am I sufficiently prepared to deal with the problems that lie ahead? Maybe I should be studying something else. And if I fail or 'screw up', what will people say? I'm really being presumptuous!"

For some, the thought of missing their calling and the resulting psychological suffering is enough to move them to action.

In moments of doubt or procrastination, it's a good idea to turn the problem around and say to yourself, "What would become of me if I didn't pursue the dream of my life? I'd always regret not having at least tried! I can't imagine just going about my routine and not satisfying the restless passion in me!" For some, the thought of missing their calling and the resulting psychological suffering is enough to move them to action. The price for refusing your mission will be nostalgia, boredom, melancholy, a feeling of emptiness, silent depression, discontent, unfulfilled hopes. In his book *Awaken the Giant Within*, Anthony Robbins states convincingly, "Becoming aware of pain is the ultimate tool for shifting a belief."

Laurie Beth Jones holds that the thought of not realizing your life's dream serves as a "point of power" for greater risk-taking. In my view, it all depends on the individual's personality: while some will be seduced by the prospect of

Impatience and haste can only lead to bitter setbacks and discouragement.

accomplishing their personal mission, others will be more motivated by the fear of missing their calling. In my own experience, both dynamics were present, but I think the passion to follow my mission was stronger than my fear of failing in it.

DON'T RUSH HEADLONG INTO YOUR MISSION, BUT DO TAKE CALCULATED RISKS

Every long journey begins with a single step.

ANONYMOUS

A danger sometimes awaits those launching into the pursuit of their dream. Under the influence of their enlightenment and carried away by their enthusiasm, they believe they can achieve success overnight. They interpret their first signs of success to mean they have become celebrities. They develop an inflated ego. I am thinking of those writers who expect that their first manuscript will be considered "brilliant," those amateur painters who want to exhibit in a famous art gallery, those who, after two weeks of training, call themselves "gurus." Their impatience and haste can only lead to bitter setbacks and discouragement. We progress one small step at a time, with perseverance, courage, patience and discernment.

In contrast to those who go rushing ahead, some dare not take the first step. They get lost in researching and analyzing; they seek the advice of experts; they take courses; they are always preparing, while what they need to do is take the plunge.

The important thing is to get moving and put your whole heart into it. At the time of the publication of my first book, *To Love Again* [published in a revised edition entitled *How to Love*

Again in 2001], I was giving many talks on the importance of going through the grief process. I was facilitating workshops on this theme and giving training sessions for various groups of specialists. I got the idea of writing a book on grieving. Just the thought of writing paralyzed me. I could see my old French teacher reading my compositions out loud in class and making fun of my stilted prose. Nevertheless, I became obsessed with the idea of writing about grief. So randomly I began to jot down on separate pieces of paper what I knew about and what I had experienced on the subject. One day I decided to assemble all my reflections and make them into a pamphlet. Then I asked some friends to read it, just to find out if it was a useful document.

While waiting for their verdict, I suffered real torment; I was full of uncertainty and doubt. To my great satisfaction, I received enthusiastic feedback. Some of my "reviewers" even completed my poems with a few verses of their own. I had reached them! Strengthened by their encouragement, I began to sell the pamphlet to people who attended my lectures. One evening, after a lecture, a friend who owned a small publishing house expressed interest in publishing my pamphlet. That was the beginning of my "hesitant writer's adventure." The photocopies of my first writings have today become a book translated into six languages and sold around the world.

This experience taught me to build my mission gradually. I should add that some missions require a huge self-investment right at the start: you cannot clear a crevasse in two leaps.

Some missions require a huge self-investment right at the start.

Sometimes the way we are tested is determined by the very nature of the calling we have chosen.

EXPECT TO BE TESTED ON YOUR MISSION JOURNEY

In myths and legends, all heroes called to great exploits meet obstacles along their path: giants and wicked witches, mermaids and monsters, mountains that defy climbing, attractions that distract them from their mission, and so on. Similarly, when we answer our call, we must expect to be tested. The solidity of our project will be put to the test.

We will also find that we must detach ourselves from certain things. Some of these detachments are expected, others unexpected. Often, we must sacrifice security, social standing, leisure time, the approval of parents or friends, financial freedom, etc. The verb "to sacrifice," from the Latin *sacrum facere*, "to do something sacred," takes on its full meaning here. We give up certain "goods" for a superior good. For the sacrifices we accept, we shall be rewarded with the "golden fleece" of our mission.

In addition to our voluntary detachments, other unexpected renunciations must be made. They may result from illness, accident, misunderstanding, being let down by someone we trusted, "bureaucratic red tape" and so forth. I encountered these kinds of obstacles when, at the age of 42, I decided to pursue studies in clinical psychology in San Francisco. The will to succeed in becoming a trained psychologist allowed me to overcome all the obstacles. Today I understand much better Nietzsche's statement that when we have a "why" that serves as our goal, we can endure any "how." The need to answer the call of our soul allows us to find within ourselves energies and resources we never knew we had.

Sometimes the way we are tested is determined by the very nature of the calling we have chosen. An elderly doctor told me about the disillusionment he experienced at the beginning of his career. His dream had been to take care of the sick and save them from death, but his assignment was to take bodies down to the morgue. He was sickened by the sight of the cold and lifeless corpses on stone slabs. He was about to give it all up. But the thought that he was part of a long line of doctors who had also had to take their turn at carrying out these dull tasks gave him the courage to persevere.

Then there was the case of the pregnant woman who, after experiencing moments of great joy, became panic-stricken at the prospect of giving birth. She feared she would not be able to handle the pain, that she might die, that her child might be deformed or stillborn. To overcome these fears, she began to think of all the women who had gone before her and who had overcome the same physical and psychological torments. This reflection reconciled her to the challenges and risks of motherhood.

This doctor and this mother-to-be found their strength and courage in considering the great archetypal images that lived within them. They connected with the power of the myth of the healer and the myth of the universal mother, thus becoming aware that they were no longer living their adventure alone, but in connection with the rest of humanity.

FEAR OF HOW OTHERS WILL REACT

The opinion of others is an important factor in determining whether you will persevere in your mission or abandon it. The possibility of being rejected by those close to you reawakens old childhood fears of being abandoned. Quite often the decision to pursue our mission frightens and upsets parents and other family members. The examples are numerous: a father decides to give up a lucrative job to pursue his passion; a mother who has stayed home with her young children wants

Quite often the decision to pursue our mission frightens and upsets parents and other family members.

To follow your mission, you may even have to leave your group.

to go back to school to have a career; a woman wants to marry a man her parents don't approve of; a man who is not interested in following in his father's footsteps embraces other plans for his life. It is difficult to go against the expectations of other members of your family. They express their disagreement in various ways: they may become distant, withdrawn, sarcastic or even threatening. But the price you must pay to realize your soul's desire is never too high, even if people disagree with you or fail to understand you.

All institutions, whether they be family, school, government, military, religious or other, share the tendency to reward submissiveness and conformity rather than independence and originality. Nothing works as strongly against the realization of a new mission. The guardians of tradition, order and stability view unfavourably those who follow their inner voice. Paradoxically, the original thinkers, initiators, inventors, creators and artists move forward the very institutions that had "excommunicated" them by breaking old taboos and obsolete laws. It does not always win me friends when I tell my students that in mid-life, we should be less obedient to the will of our superiors than to the call of our deepest desires.

To follow your mission, you may even have to leave your group because it is too difficult to tolerate remarks like, "Who does he think he is, changing jobs just like that? What a dabbler! He can't stick to anything." Being ready to follow your call also means being willing to face suspicion or aggressivity from those who did not have the courage to follow theirs. When you disturb the conformist peace of a milieu or group, you ruin the well-established image that others have of themselves. Losing your reputation as a "good guy" or a "nice gal" is sometimes the price you pay for realizing your soul's dream. You must know how to handle this visceral fear rooted in the sensitivity of the child in us: that is, how to deal with the fear of disapproval and social rejection.

It is frightening to say "yes" to our mission, because this obliges us to choose our true friends. Happy are those who can count on the encouragement of at least one person who believes in them and their mission. As I was about to undertake my psychology studies, I received the unconditional support of my local superior. He may not have known it but, in my darkest hours, his words gave me the courage to continue.

When you are about to carry out your mission, you must learn to recognize the naysayers, the "prophets of doom," and not allow them into your space.

FIND THE RIGHT PEOPLE TO WORK WITH

One day I confided to a friend that I wanted to publish a second book that year. He advised me not to do it, claiming that it showed an offensive seeking of popularity as well as an excessive desire to earn money. At first, I was somewhat shocked by his remarks. Then, I quickly put them out of my mind and went on with my writing project. When you are about to carry out your mission, you must learn to recognize the naysayers, the "prophets of doom," and not allow them into your space. In fact, the advice they give says more about their own fear, even their jealousy, than about their desire to help.

To accomplish your mission, the ability to ask for help is also a precious asset. Often, due to shyness or a misplaced spirit of independence, we dare not solicit the help of others. It is a trait of North American culture to want to go it alone, to boast when we succeed by ourselves, and to be able to say, à la Frank Sinatra, "I did it my way." Therefore, it is important for someone embracing a big project to sit down and draw up a list of everything they will need: material resources, knowledge, collaborators, encouragement, etc.

Once you have answered your call, your small inner voice will ask you to continue to honour the dream of your soul.

Once the list is complete, you will be in a position to determine those tasks you can carry out alone and those for which you will need help from someone else. Not to ask for help is the surest way not to get any. On the other hand, if you dare ask for it, you will almost certainly get it. In fact, most people feel honoured to be trusted this way.

We seek special qualities in our collaborators. They, too, must believe in our project, even be excited about it. However, it is important that they retain a certain amount of detachment. We are not looking for a relationship of dependence, but of respectful interdependence, similar to that of mentor and disciple. Furthermore, it is preferable to choose collaborators who are carrying out their own mission, people who know the way for having travelled it and who can therefore lend their precious experience and practical advice. To edit my books, I found the ideal mentor: he is interested in my work, corrects my writing, points out where clarity is lacking, challenges certain statements, suggests improvements and rejoices in my successes.

RENEW YOUR COMMITMENT CONSTANTLY

Don't think that once your mission is accomplished, there is nothing else left for you to do in life. In fact, once you have answered your call, you will find it more and more difficult to silence your small inner voice. It will ask you to continue to honour the dream of your soul. It will still pursue you after your initial successes. Constantly turned towards the future, it will not let you look back. It will give you no respite: it will direct you towards other challenges, like reaching a larger number of people and having a deeper influence on them.

When I look back over my calling as a communicator motivating people to help themselves, I discover that my mission has reached wider horizons than I had first anticipated.

I began as a psychotherapist, went on to facilitate small groups, then became a writer, teaching people how to help themselves. Despite my shyness, I began by saying "yes" when I was invited to speak to small groups. I renewed my "yes" when I was asked to address large audiences or to grant interviews to the media: newspapers, radio and television. My first "yes's" have led to my giving training workshops in Europe. What still remains for me to undertake? Create a web site? Establish a centre for the training of professionals? Write other books further developing the themes already tackled? The end of my mission does not yet seem to be in sight.

VISUALIZE THE OBSTACLES YOU MUST OVERCOME

Sometimes, just the thought of seeing your mission accomplished raises all kinds of fears. You imagine obstacles along your path. Illusion or reality? To find out, here is a visualization exercise that will enable you to look them squarely in the eye and find the means to befriend them.

• Reread the ideal vision of your mission. If you find it is still not precise enough, add whatever further details are needed.

Slowly, enter your inner self. Close your eyes if necessary. Listen to the noises and sounds around you, and enter more deeply into your inner self.

Become aware of your breathing, your inhaling ... and exhaling. This will enable you to become even more inwardly focused.

Shake out the tensions in your body. Slowly breathe out your fatigue. Feel your body relax.

Now imagine a symbol that could represent your mission. It might be a person, an object, an animal, a landscape or something else. Surround this being with light and place it on a raised surface. Take time to contemplate it seriously.

Next, contemplate the path that leads to your symbol.

Take time to imagine it clearly.

Along this path you see, hear and feel the presence of rather bizarre beings. They flank either side of the path to prevent you from accomplishing your mission.

During this time, in the very depths of yourself, renew your desire and your will to travel the path that separates you from the object of your dreams. Keep your eyes fixed on the splendour of the symbol of your mission that you placed on the raised surface.

On one side of the road, you meet creatures that try to distract you. They show you other directions. They beckon you to follow them. Imagine the things and the activities they present to seduce and distract you from the path of your mission.

On the other side of the road are creatures who try to frighten you. Imagine what they are saying to discourage you from making progress. "You're not capable ... you won't make it ... you have neither the courage nor the perseverance you need to reach your goal ... just drop it ... it's too difficult ..." You can even identify the individuals who might say such things to you.

Still farther along, you see the prophets of doom. Listen to what they say.

Other people on the path dread your success; they are afraid that you will change too much for their liking, that they won't recognize you anymore. Consequently, they want to dissuade you from pursuing your mission. They threaten to leave you. Who are these people?

You also meet people who mock you and ridicule your project. What do you say to them? One good strategy is quite simply to ignore them.

Next you meet people who try to seduce you and distract you from your mission. You imagine them trying to scatter your energy.
You stop to dialogue with some of your adversaries. But others aren't even worth the delay.

With every obstacle you meet, you continue to concentrate on your mission. You feel courageous, strong and enthusiastic.

All these sinister characters only make you double your inner determination to accomplish your mission.

Finally, having arrived at the symbol of your mission, you take time to actually take possession of it. You savour your victory, and let feelings of pride and satisfaction well up within you. You toss a quick glance back over all the obstacles you encountered and congratulate yourself on your courage, skill and perseverance. These feelings will continue to motivate you in the days, weeks, months and years ahead.

Gradually, you return to the world around you at your own pace. Slowly you open your eyes. You feel calm, relaxed and proud of yourself.

✛ ✛ ✛

The realization of your mission is contagious.

The story of Jonah had a happy ending. From the moment he accepted his mission, the tempest at sea subsided. He preached to the people of Nineveh, who received the light and were converted. Even God changed – abandoning revenge in favour of compassion on the Ninevites. Jonah's "yes" had an influence beyond the limits of his personal drama; it made itself felt throughout his entire surroundings.

The dialogue consisting of calls and responses to your mission places you in direct contact with the depths of your Self, the intimate God of your soul, and, through a mysterious alchemy, with the community around you as well. The realization of your mission is contagious, for it creates an invisible, but very real, field of energy. Once you have accepted your mission, others will wake from their stupor and their existential void, allow their soul's dream to rise up within them and begin to believe in *their* mission.

Journal of My Discoveries about My Mission

Why Keep a Journal?

At this point in your reading, you may be wondering just how far you have gotten in your search for your mission. This chapter will help you take stock of your discoveries. In particular, it will help you to compile the results of the exercises, put them in order and, finally, focus your mission statement more sharply.

This summary of your findings follows the same outline as the related chapters.

Part Two:
The Letting Go Phase

I. Saying my goodbyes (Chapter 4)

Different kinds of goodbyes

At what stage of transition do I find myself now? What foreseeable losses have I confronted?

Losses faced in childhood:

Losses related to adolescence:

Losses arising in mid-life:

Losses at retirement:

Losses that come with old age:

Losses due to illness or disability:

Others:

What unforeseeable, accidental losses have I had to deal with?

Accidents:

Layoff or unemployment:

Divorce or disappointment in love:

Bankruptcy:

Loss of reputation:

Other:

What indicators tell me that a change is underway in my life?

Boredom, feeling of emptiness and meaninglessness:

Nostalgia, depression, uneasiness:

Feeling of guilt at missing my goal in life:

Physical symptoms that are hard to explain medically:

Daydreams about what I could have accomplished:

What stage of grieving am I in now?

— Am I in the midst of the shock and denial of my loss?
— Am I allowing myself to live my emotions and my feelings: powerlessness, fear, sadness, anger, sorrow, liberation, awareness that it is all really over?

— Am I ready to assert my loss and start settling certain matters: for example, to get rid of useless items, to complete transactions, to separate myself from what no longer is, and so on?

— Following the loss I have undergone, am I at the point of finding meaning to my life and envisioning a special mission that flows out of the drama I have just experienced?

— Can I forgive myself for the shortcomings in my love and forgive others for having left me?

— Am I in the process of harvesting the legacy of all the love, effort and energy I poured out while I was attached to the one I loved or to what I loved?

II. Healing that lets me rediscover my mission (Chapter 5)

My wounds

What major wounds must I heal in order to regain my self-confidence?

Forgiveness: the steps involved
What steps of forgiveness have I gone through?

I have finished with the idea of revenge:

I am becoming more aware of my injury:

I am talking about it to my offender or to someone I trust:

I have clearly identify the wounded part of my being so I can grieve my loss:

I am overcoming my inclinations towards revenge and aggressiveness:

I forgive myself for having let myself be aggressive and for continuing to hurt myself:

I understand my offender:

I am giving meaning to my life after my injury:

I renounce any feeling of moral superiority that the act of forgiveness might give me:

I leave everything up to the love of the God who forgave me and who gives me the strength to forgive:

In my heart I am reconciled with my offender and reflect on whether it is prudent to build a new relationship with him or her:

My mission

Am I able to find clues to my mission in the meaning my life has begun to take on following a bereavement or serious injury?

Sign of a mission ensuing from my grief and my wounds:

Part Three – The Neutral Zone
(The Liminal Phase)

I. Identifying my shadow (Chapter 6)

I summarize my discoveries and describe those aspects of my shadow I discovered in myself after questioning myself about my shadow.

How well have I succeeded in befriending my shadow and integrating it so that I feel greater inner harmony?

II. Seeking my identity (Chapter 7)

Many ask themselves what is their true identity, the nature of their deepest Self. As I have already said, the more we shed our superficial identities – either following an involuntary loss or through disidentification exercises – the more the Self emerges.

What were the results of the two disidentification exercises? What did I become aware of?

Searching for the symbols that best define me

I summarize here the results obtained from the exercises I did to discover my identity.

Exercise 1
The stories that brought delight to my childhood, my adolescence and my adult life:

I.
2.
3.

Exercise 2
What moral qualities are present in my "heroes" and "heroines"?

Exercise 3
With what historical or mythical figure, animal or plant did I identify?

Describe how this entity partially defines me.

Exercise 4
Describe the qualities that make me a unique person.

III. Strategies for discovering my mission (Chapter 8)

The story of my life reveals my future

After you went back over your personal story, you observed certain things that were constant: actions, attitudes, positions taken, ways of relating and deciding. This information helped you define the archetypes that live within you. Name these archetypes by describing succinctly how they influenced your life.

Have I found in my story recurrent themes that might give me clues about my mission?

Did I identify with certain archetypes? Which ones?

Archetype 1:

Archetype 2:

The intuitions of adolescence
Who were the heroes/heroines in whom I discerned signs announcing my own mission? What were their missions?

My eulogy
I summarize briefly the principal traits of my personality and mission as they were described in the eulogy at my funeral:

Conclusion
With the data you have gathered in this chapter, you can begin to describe certain parameters of your mission.

IV. My passion, my mission (Chapter 9)
At this point, read your last tentative mission statement, as drawn up in Chapter 9. Look at it in light of all you have discovered and all the information you acquired. Add to the wording of your mission statement the qualities that justify the statement and the context in which you would like to carry it out.

My third mission statement:

V. How the universe calls us (Chapter 10)

Metaphors I use to describe my mission and my vision of life and the world:

I am attentive to the messages the universe sends me (synchronicity):

I remember the messages I received from certain "prophets"/mentors:

Summary of the liminal stage

Take the time now to observe the coherence between your mission statement and all the information that you have gathered. Ask yourself, for instance, "Is my mission statement in harmony with my world-view, with the meaning I have given my life following the losses I have undergone, with the messages I have received from people who are important to me? Is it in keeping with the symbols that I identified with, in keeping with my principal archetype, with the personality traits I discovered in my funeral eulogy...?"

If so, it would seem that your mission statement translates the authentic aspiration of your soul. If, on the other hand, there is very little correspondence between your mission statement and the information you gathered, ask yourself what corrections need to be made.

Part Four: The New Beginning
I. My ideal vision: a detailed description of my mission (Chapter 11)

If there are intermediate ideal visions, what are they?

First intermediate ideal vision:

Second intermediate ideal vision:

II. Ways I resist accomplishing my mission (Chapter 12)

Nostalgia:

Acting rashly:
Doubting the authenticity of my mission:

Indecision even when the vision of my mission is clear:

Fear of resistance from my acquaintances:

Fear of rejection by my family and friends:

I am willing to be "tested"

List of "false prophets" to avoid

List of people who might be good to work with

Anticipating how my mission could expand

BIBLIOGRAPHY

Adrienne, C. *The Purpose of your Life.* New York: Eagle Brook, 1998.

Bach, R. *Illusions: The Adventures of a Reluctant Messiah.* New York: Bantam, 1998.

Billington, A. et al. (Eds.) *Mission and Meaning: Essays Presented to Peter Cotterell.* Carlisle, U.K.: Paternoster Press, 1995.

Bolles, R. N. *How to Find Your Mission in Life.* Berkeley: Ten Speed Press, 1991.

————.*What Colour Is Your Parachute?: A Practical Manual for Job-Hunters and Career Changers.* Berkeley: Ten Speed Press, 1995.

Brewi, J. and Anne Brennan. *Mid-Life: Psychological and Spiritual Perspectives.* New York: Crossroad, 1982.

Bridges, W. *Transitions: Making Sense of Life's Changes.* Menlo Park, CA: Addison-Wesley, 1996.

Cameron, J. *The Vein of Gold: A Journey to Your Creative Heart.* New York: Tarcher/Putnam, 1997.

Campbell, J. with Bill Moyers. *The Power of Myth.* New York: Doubleday, 1988.

Christus, Pratiques ignatiennes: donner et recevoir les Exercises spirituels [Christus, Ignatian practices: directing and following the Spiritual Exercises]. May 1996, No. 170. See particularly the chapter on "election" starting on page 180.

Cochran, L. R. *The Sense of Vocation: A Study of Career and Life Development.* Albany: State University of New York Press, 1990.

Coelho, P. *The Alchemist: A Fable About Following Your Dream.* New York: HarperFlamingo, 1998. Translated from the original Portuguese (Brazil, 1988) by Alan R. Clarke.

Covey, S. *The Seven Habits of Highly Effective People: Restoring the Character Ethic.* New York: Simon and Schuster, 1990.

Daudet, A. *Lettres de mon moulin.* Paris: Nelson, 1942.

Enright, R. D. and Joanna North (Eds.). *Exploring Forgiveness.* Madison: University of Wisconsin Press, 1998.

Frankl, V. E. *Man's Search for Meaning: An Introduction to Logotherapy.* New York: Washington Square Press, 1965.

Gennep, A. van. *The Rites of Passage.* Chicago: University of Chicago Press, 1969.

Haineault, P. *Comment tirer profit des bouleversements de sa vie.* Outremont: Quebecor, 1997.

Hillman, J. *The Soul's Code: In Search of Character and Calling.* New York: Random House, 1996.

Johnson, R. *He: Understanding Masculine Psychology.* New York: Harper and Row, 1974.

Jones, L. B. *The Path: Creating Your Mission Statement for Work and for Life.* New York: Hyperion, 1996.

Jung, C. J. *Memories, Dreams and Reflections.* New York: Vintage, 1989.

Keen, S. and Anne Valley-Fox. *Your Mythic Journey: Finding Meaning in Your Life Through Writing and Storytelling.* Los Angeles: Jeremy P. Tarcher, 1989.

Kornfield, J. *A Path with Heart: A Guide Through the Perils and Promises of Spiritual Life.* New York: Bantam, 1993.

Levoy, G. *Callings: Finding and Following an Authentic Life.* New York: Random House, 1998.

McCarthy, K. W. *The On-Purpose Person: How to Discover, Clarify and Achieve Your Life Purpose.* Colorado Springs: Nav Press, 1992.

McNally, D. *Even Eagles Need a Push: Learning to Soar in a Changing World.* Toronto: Dell Distributing, 1994.

Menuhin, Y. *Unfinished Journey.* London: MacDonald and Jane's Publishers, 1976.

Monbourquette, J. et al. *Je suis aimable, je suis capable: parcours pour l'estime et l'affirmation de soi.* Outremont: Novalis, 1996 (Part VI, Chapter 9).

Monbourquette, J. *How to Befriend Your Shadow: Welcoming Your Unloved Side.* Ottawa: Novalis, 2001.

How to Forgive: A Step-by-Step Guide. Ottawa/Cincinnati/London:
  Novalis/St. Anthony Messenger Press/Darton, Longman and
  Todd, 2000.

How to Love Again: Moving from Grief to Growth. Ottawa/Mystic, CT:
Novalis/Twenty-Third Publications, 2001.
  (Revised edition of *To Love Again: Finding Comfort and
  Meaning in Times of Grief,* 1993.)

Pacot, S. *L'évangélisation des profondeurs.* Paris: Cerf, 1997.

Pauchant, T.C. et al. *La quête du sens.* Montreal: Québec/Amérique,
  1996 (in particular, the article by Estelle Morin, "L'efficacité
  organisationnelle et le sens du travail", pp. 257-288).

Pearce, Joseph Chilton. *Evolution's End: Claiming the Potential of Our
  Intelligence.* Toronto: HarperCollins, 1993.

Robbins, A. *Awaken the Giant Within.* New York: Simon and Schuster,
  1992.

Roberge, M. *Tant d'hiver au coeur du changement.* Sainte-Foy: Editions
  Septembre, 1998.

Sher, B. *I Could Do Anything If I Only Knew What It Was: How to Discover
  What You Really Want and How to Get It.* New York: Delacorte Press,
  1994.

Spangler, D. *The Call.* New York: Riverhead Books, 1996.

———.*Everyday Miracles: The Inner Art of Manifestation.* New York:
  Bantam, 1996.

Stephan, N. *Fulfill Your Soul's Purpose: Ten Creative Paths to Your Life Mission.*
  Walpole, NH: Stillpoint Publishing, 1994.

Tetlow, J.A. *Choosing Christ in the World: Directing the Spiritual Exercises of St.
  Ignatius Loyola According to Annotations Eighteen and Nineteen, A Handbook.*
  Saint Louis, Missouri: The Institute of Jesuit Sources, 1989.

Viorst, J. *Necessary Losses.* New York: Simon and Schuster, 1998.

ALSO BY JOHN MONBOURQUETTE

HOW TO BEFRIEND YOUR SHADOW
Welcoming Your Unloved Side

Each of us has a "shadow," composed of everything we have driven back into our unconscious for fear of being rejected by the people we loved when we were young. Over the years, we created a whole underground world filled with things that were shameful, displeasing or upsetting to those around us.

Our task as adults is to rediscover what makes up our shadow, to bring it into the light, and to use it for our own spiritual growth. If we refuse to do this work, we risk being out of balance psychologically, and our lives and relationships will not reach their fullest potential.

Is your shadow your friend or your enemy? That will depend on how you see it and how you relate to it. This book offers you the tools you need to welcome your shadow side. Befriend your shadow, and watch your relationship with yourself and with others grow and deepen!

• 160 pages
• paperback

HOW TO FORGIVE
A Step-By-Step Guide

"What does it take to forgive?" asks John Monbourquette, best-selling author, psychologist and priest. His answer is a unique twelve-step guide which offers profound and practical advice on overcoming the emotional, spiritual and psychological blocks to true forgiveness.

Monbourquette begins by exploring the nature of forgiveness and exploding some of the myths. He shows how essential forgiveness is for us all, whatever our beliefs, for forgiveness touches on all aspects of the human person, the biological and psychological as well as the spiritual. He then takes the reader through his twelve-step healing process, providing practical exercises, case histories, anecdotes and even poetry along the way.

How to Forgive is an honest and touching book that unlocks the liberating and transformative power of forgiveness.
• 200 pages
• paperback

HOW TO LOVE AGAIN
Moving From Grief to Growth

Are you suffering from a deep loss in your life? *How to Love Again* is a book that can offer you comfort in a time of despair. It is intended to accompany you on the journey you are about to make. You may want to read it from cover to cover, meditate on it, or refer back to those passages that most inspire you.

Author John Monbourquette describes the kind of healing that comes after loss: "In the same way the physical body deals with a physical wound, the emotional body begins a healing process the moment the emotional trauma occurs. Allow the natural wisdom of your healing system to come to your rescue. Eventually the pain will subside, and you will then be more aware of life around you, more open to happiness, more fully human once again."

"Throughout this journey, I would like you to face your pain and to recognize it peacefully. This attitude will help you survive. It will facilitate your healing process and will actually help you to benefit from your own suffering.

"In this way, you will move from grief to growth, and learn how to love again."

- 168 pages
- paperback
- Revised edition, previously published as *To Love Again: Finding Comfort and Meaning in Times of Grief*